Hw 2 ★t ur Fmly Hstry

by

Jane Starkie

THE FAMILY HISTORY PARTNERSHIP

Published by
The Family History Partnership
PO Box 502
Bury, Lancashire BL8 9EP

Copyright © Jane Starkie

ISBN: 978 1 906280 04 8

First published 2008

Printed and bound by Alden HenDi
De Havilland Way, Witney, Oxon OX29 0YG

Contents

Preface   4

Foreword   7

Introduction: In the beginning   9

Chapter 1: Once upon a time   16

Chapter 2: Leaves on the tree   33

Chapter 3: B4ubgn — get connected   44

Chapter 4: Hatched, matched and despatched   52

Civil registration   66

Parish registers   67

Chapter 5: Taking the register   68

The National Archives (TNA)   78

Chapter 6: Tinker, tailor, soldier, sailor . . .   81

Chapter 7: Rich man, poor man, beggar man, thief . . .   94

Chapter 8: What's in a name?   111

Chapter 9: Every picture tells a story   126

Chapter 10: This is your life!   142

Time-line snake   152

Suggested further reading   154

Bibliography   156

Address book   157

Answers to puzzles   158

Preface

This is the place in a book to look on as a sort of notice board.

It is here that people are thanked for their help and encouragement. There are many that I thank and they will all know who they are, perhaps with the exception of the schoolboy whom I grabbed coming out of the dentists' loo to inspect the badge on his blazer. He must have really wondered what planet I was from! Although I give everybody a big thank you, there are a few names that deserve a special mention.

Firstly, what might have encouraged you to pick this book up in the first place is the cover. The artist Brian Gough produced this one for me within a few days for which I am very grateful.

Brett Langston, Joyce Finnemore, Lynda Raistrick and Peter Watson have all kindly spent some time proof reading and editing.

ABM Publishing (who publish *Family Tree* Magazine and *Practical Family History*), well known to many family historians, have been extremely generous in allowing me access to their picture library.

I hope you will agree that Vicky Simons was a real star to devote a whole day of her half term in reading the whole script and going through the pictures with me. She has also given help and suggestions, and sketched some delightful illustrations. Georgina Feather has kindly spent an afternoon reading everything through very carefully.

It is fairly common to put picture acknowledgements at the front or end of a book, but I have chosen to put them underneath the relevant illustrations instead. I thank all those who very kindly gave me permission to reproduce their own illustrations. Every effort has been made to trace the owners of all the copyright material. If anyone has been overlooked, firstly accept my apologies and then please inform me.

Not only did Eddie Stobart Ltd, the well-known road-haulage company, give kind permission to reproduce their logo, but they also named two of their lorries after my daughters.

I thank Pauline Litton who is possibly more responsible for this book than others. She was my teacher who inspired me with the love of history all those years ago. She then introduced me to family history and subsequently encouraged me when I first suggested the idea of a book for children.

I also thank the well-known author Pamela Oldfield who very kindly wrote the Foreword.

Finally, my grateful thanks go to my family, my brother-in-law and Bob Boyd, the publisher, who has had to put up with me for what to him must feel like a very long time!

In Chapter 5, I have taken the liberty of ever so slightly changing the wording of St Luke's Gospel in the New Testament of the Bible. This was to make it easier for you to understand the context of this chapter on censuses.

I have spent a considerable amount of time in my local library. As well as borrowing books on subjects like flags and poetry, I was frequently to be seen in the children's section. Some of the books that I have listed at the end as suggested further reading are fictional. This means that the actual stories and names were not entirely true in real life, but they were in fact woven around **very real** events. Some of the titles recommended will help to give you a clearer picture and understanding of both World Wars. All of them are very sad in places, so if really sad things upset you perhaps you should not read them yet. Alternatively, make sure that you have a box of tissues to hand … so you have been warned.

In the text I say that when compiling a family tree always start with yourself and work backwards. However, for the example of a family tree on page 39 in Chapter 2 I chose my daughter Hannah as the *star* instead of myself. I decided that reproducing her tree would introduce Irish as well as English and Scottish ancestors. Both her dad's parents were born in Ireland (her dad is my husband John). Showing my family tree would have certainly illustrated my Scottish ancestors, but nobody from Ireland.

My grandmother (Annie Florence Manley) was born in Wales; but so far I have found no Welsh ancestry (certainly nothing has been found — yet!). For this reason I selected her birth certificate as an example of an illustration of a certificate.

Finally to be able to do the puzzles without spoiling your book, you might want to photocopy, and possibly enlarge, the relevant pages. You will discover that many answers can be found somewhere in the book.

I now leave you to read on . . .

Jane Starkie

There once was a schoolgirl called Kate
Who went out on a date with a mate,
Not chill out at a movie –
To appear wicked n' groovy ...
... But to check on her ancestor's fate.

To start the task, it was simple to ask
The wrinklies before it's too late;
'Cos while they still live –
The answers they give
Could provide her wait ... with a 'great-great'.

Let's consider birth, marriage n' death –
From the first to the very last breath
Thus solving the mystery ...
Of her own family history ...
Whether looking for a Percy or a Beth.

With help from Debbie

KATE

Keep careful notes
Ask lots of questions
Tell someone where u r going
Enjoy

"As you get older your roots become more important to you"
Diane Abbott MP

6

Dedication

This book is dedicated to all babies and children who have never had, nor will have the chance to grow up. They will never be able to know, nor will they have the opportunity of finding out about their family history.

Foreword

If you are interested in family history, this book will inspire you. The well-researched chapters will send you in search of your lost relatives, both good and bad! These strangers will be related to you through strong family ties, even though some of them may have lived and died long before you were born.

As a writer of historical novels, I know the pleasures of researching, and envy you your 'time travel' into the past. One day you may find yourself poring over old photographs with a magnifying glass, or tracking down yellowing newspaper cuttings — or even, if you are lucky, reading an old diary filled with the hopes and fears of someone long dead. All of these, and more, will offer clues to the hidden lives of members of your family.

We live in an eventful present, and face an exciting future, but Jane Starkie's lively, fact-filled pages will help you take amazing glimpses into an equally exciting place — the intriguing world of past lives.

PAMELA OLDFIELD

With thanks to Troon Family History Society, Ayrshire, for permission to reproduce the tree.

INTRODUCTION

In the beginning

As I write this, family history is the fastest-growing hobby among adults. I see no reason why it cannot be just as popular with younger family members. One of the first problems is the lack of books to attract you important people to this very absorbing, fascinating and rewarding pastime. I say important people because you younger family members will be part of the adult population of the future. All our knowledge of today will be passed on to you.

My main aim in this book is to generate enough interest in the subject of family history. If you enjoy detective stories, mazes, jigsaw puzzles and are interested in history — particularly your own — I reckon that you are a good candidate. Just like a detective story, you have a 'crime' and need to solve the mystery with the clues that you have. Each time you discover something new it becomes another completed piece of your very own puzzle — and this can sometimes be very exciting.

I am not planning to go into too much of the detail as to how to trace your ancestors. I want to get you interested in anything and everything that is old, whilst you continue to appear to your friends as the 'with it, cool dude' that you are. No I do not mean 'the wrinklies' when I mention old!

You could even consider doing your family tree with a friend. You'll obviously be climbing up different trees, but you would be working together with ideas, outings and experiences.

I'm going to sound just like a parent for a moment here! Reminding you that if you are spending money that is not yours (e.g. the land-line phone and the internet), it would be polite to always get permission first and then you shouldn't be grumbled at later on. To start with, family history will be very inexpensive, but as you make progress it will probably begin to cost more. I'm sorry to sound like a nagging parent, but always tell an adult where you are planning to go.

" Where do I come from?" This must be a question asked by most children at some time during their first years. We think we know exactly what the child is thinking when asking that, but look further into the question and suddenly many more come to mind, for example 'What is history?' 'What is family history?' and 'Why are we doing this?' I even looked up the word 'history' in the dictionary (definitely uncool). 'Whatever happened in the past' is history, whether it happened yesterday, last week, last year or a hundred years ago. Everyone has ancestors — you may be trendy, sporty, funky and drop dead gorgeous, but what about your past? Surely some modern, young people in the world today would love to learn more about what happened to their family, before they themselves were even thought of — or a twinkle in their father's eye ;-)

You may want to know if there was anyone famous amongst your ancestors. Were your ancestors rich, poor, in the army, in the navy, 'in service', working on the land, or even owning the land?

'In service' is just an old-fashioned way of saying a servant. I know two ladies who remember being 'in domestic service', working in big houses for families that had lots of money.

You may have noticed that sometimes when 'new faces' in the world of show business with an interesting past come onto the scene, the newspapers very quickly have their family trees (or pedigrees as they can also be called) drawn up and printed for us all to see. We only need to go back to the first person to win a million pounds on the TV show, *Who Wants to Be a Millionaire?* This first winner is descended from King Edward the Seventh, and her family tree was reproduced in many of the daily papers the following day. Likewise, since the engagement and marriage of Prince Charles and Camilla Parker-Bowles, we have seen both their family trees printed in various newspapers.

FUN AND INTERESTING WEBSITE
Museum of Childhood . . .
www.museumofchildhood.org.uk

At the time of writing, history seems to be making a fashionable comeback. There are quite a few history programmes on TV at the moment and I know that the *Horrible Histories* are making quite a hit with schoolchildren. *Past Times*, a popular shop in many towns and shopping centres, sells goods with historical themes and connections. Since 2004 we have been entertained with a variety of well-known personalities tracing their family histories in the BBC Television series, *Who Do You Think You Are?*, with more to follow.

In February 2005, *Blue Peter* viewers were treated to a canter around Norfolk where one of the presenters comes from. Part of the programme included him beginning to research his family tree. At the end he said, "I would thoroughly recommend looking into your family tree, because you never know who or what you might discover".

2002 was a particularly good year for events that will be well recorded, and go down in history as historical moments. Although very sad, the Queen Mother's lying-in-state and funeral on April 9th was a magnificent occasion. It was said many times on both radio and TV by the commentators that "We are watching history in the making" and "History was made today". Yes, true, but history is being made every day.

In the same year her daughter Queen Elizabeth II (the Second) celebrated her Golden Jubilee. This meant that she had been Queen for 50 years, after her father King George the Sixth died in February 1952. The Union Flag, which is the flag of Great Britain (also called the United Kingdom or UK), was seen fluttering from many buildings for weeks, and there were all sorts of events taking place all over the country as part of the celebration.

The Dangerous Book for Boys by Conn and Hal Iggulden shows how the design of this flag came about. Reproduced courtesy of Philip's Maps and Atlases.

Some other occasions when you will see lots of flags are the Olympic Games, the Winter Olympic Games, the Commonwealth Games, Cricket Test Matches and of course the Football and Rugby World Cups.

It is a possibility that most people born British Citizens today have a very good chance of tracing their ancestors back for eight generations. A generation is the average time interval between the birth of a parent and the birth of his or her child. This is generally accepted to be 25 — 30 years.

For those born in other countries and not British Citizens, it is sometimes much harder to establish your ancestry and a far more daunting task altogether. Do not be put off by this. You may need to turn to more specialised information and help from professionals. I do not intend to go into this in any more detail here; however I would be delighted if you remain determined to try and discover some of your past.

A friend of mine used to be a teacher in Birmingham. Most of the children she taught whose ancestors originated from foreign countries, knew their fairly recent family histories. This is because they were told when very young by their parents and grandparents, and encouraged to be proud of their past.

A rather suitable Chinese proverb (saying) is, "If you want to know the future, look to the past". Yet another proverb says "If there was no past there would be no future".

Wherever you go always be on the look-out for old and interesting things.

"Snooks" at Aldeburgh, Suffolk.
Photograph: Liz Carter

12

Whatever your feelings and beliefs on some of the subjects that I have talked about, we are **all** now living in the 21st century whatever our class, colour, sex or religion. I am writing this in 2008. For the next few years, those of you that are reading this were born in the last century, and your great-grandparents may well have been born in the 19th century!

Certainly to begin with, your interests in any records will be in the 20th century. I am fairly certain that your grandparents would have been born sometime around or after the Second World War.

Hopefully this book will take you on a journey into the past and give you an idea of the life your ancestors led without TVs, PCs and mobile phones.

I know that I am not going to get everything right because you can never please everyone. For example do you prefer to be called 'children', 'kids', 'pupils', 'students', 'young people' or even 'young adults'? Some will say that a 'kid' is a young goat and an insult to children. Others will say the complete opposite and state that young adults never really experienced the innocence of childhood.

Finally, my principal reason for writing this is because for several years now I have been saying that books on family history are needed for the younger members of the family. I have often been asked if there are any suitable titles. To the best of my knowledge there are very few publications, so I feel sure that there is a gap on the shelf just waiting for a book such as this. I decided that as I was constantly saying that one should be written I ought to do something about it — so here goes . . . .

Important points to remember

- ❖ If you find that you're getting bored — please turn quickly to the next page.

- ❖ Ancestors are all the people that you are descended from.

- ❖ History is everything that took place in the past.

- ❖ Descendants are the children of generations of ancestors.

- ❖ A jubilee is a special anniversary.

- ❖ The United Kingdom (UK) or Great Britain includes England, Wales, Scotland and Northern Ireland.

- ❖ A generation is the time between the births of parents and the births of their children.

- ❖ A century is a period of 100 years.

- ❖ Remember to get permission from parents or guardians for anything you do that is using their money.

- ❖ Always tell an adult where you are going.

❖ Many people bought their first ever TV sets to watch her Coronation in 1953 — up until this time, families would sit together listening to the wireless (radio). Ask your grand-parents, uncles and aunts if they can remember listening to programmes such as *Dick Barton*, *ITMA*, *The Goon Show*, *Journey into Space* and *Much Binding in the Marsh*

❖ None of the soaps had even been thought of. Nor had programmes like *Friends*, *Big Brother*, *Pop Idol*, *Grange Hill*, *The Weakest Link*, *Who Wants to be a Millionaire?* and *Match of the Day*

❖ There was still food rationing from the Second World War — until 1954

❖ The most popular children's toy that year was the hoola-hoop

❖ David was the most popular boy's name — in 2006 it was Jack

❖ Susan was the most popular girl's name — in 2006 it was Olivia

❖ 54 years ago many families did not own a car at all, whereas today there are lots of young adults who cannot wait to buy a car as soon as they pass the Driving Test. There was no such thing as a car-boot sale and many school children would have walked to and from school

❖ Holidays abroad were mainly for rich and famous people. You just did not pop over to Paris for the weekend in 1952

❖ The Channel Tunnel and the M25 had not been built

❖ There were no credit cards known to dads as flexible friends — you paid with pounds, shillings and pence

❖ Space exploration had not yet begun. No-one had stood on the moon looking at us here on planet Earth until the first moon landing in 1969 — which was the same year that Concorde and jumbo jets came into service

❖ Boys had the *Eagle* magazine whilst the main magazine for teenage girls was *Girls Own*. Of course there were also the ever popular *Beano* and *Dandy*

❖ It was not generally realised that smoking damages your health

❖ Litter and graffiti were not nearly as bad as they are today; the recycling of waste materials had not really begun seriously

❖ Shops like Next or New Look had not arrived. Nor could you just pop into The Body Shop, Superdrug or Accessorize to get your last minute 'bits' and 'smellies' as they were not around either. Jeans had not yet become a fashion statement

❖ Mount Everest (the World's highest mountain) had not been climbed. The news that it had, reached us on the day of the Coronation ... June 2nd 1953

In 1952, the most popular toy was the hula-hoop. Photograph taken by Jimmy Forsyth of Anne in Gloucester Street, Newcastle.

ANAGRAMS

Unscramble the meaningless letters in the left column and then match them with the words in the right column. This rearranging of letters is called an anagram.

1.	LINBIGS	GENEALOGY
2.	DROCERS	GRAND PARENTS
3.	O'SHIRTY	ADOPTED
4.	PIE GREED	CENSUS
5.	NOT SCARE	DESCENDANT
6.	PANTS R DANGER	HISTORY
7.	DATE POD	RECORDS
8.	SUNSEC	ANCESTOR
9.	A LONE EGGY	SIBLING
10.	SCENTED DAN	PEDIGREE

CHAPTER ONE
Once upon a time

When I was a schoolgirl, I learnt many things. The two that come to mind at once are, firstly, my love of history which was my favourite subject. Secondly, when trying to solve a problem always work from the known to the unknown or, in other words, start with the easiest part, as you probably would when doing a jigsaw puzzle.

From this interest in history came a wish to find out more about my family from the past. As well as finding out who they were, I also wanted to find out what they did. What they played with, what they wore and whether they travelled are all questions I wanted answering. Today we take so much for granted.

Sometimes a few hours with no light except torches and candles can be great fun, but imagine spending every evening of your life with a power cut. Today it is difficult to imagine life without electricity but our ancestors managed without it for thousands of years.

A family having supper. The only light is from the fire heating the food, and the candle.

To get to school your great-great-grandparents did not climb into 'mum's taxi', share the school run with other families or catch the school bus. They would probably have walked, and very often for many miles if they lived a long way from the village school. Their parents probably did not go to school at all because most families could not afford it. The only available teaching equipment, apart from the teachers' blackboard was the piece of chalk and the slate that most pupils would have had. In fact even now I know someone who can remember having had a slate at school!

Children in the past would certainly have had nothing like modern school children, such as character lunch boxes, calculators and a pencil case stuffed with every kind of writing and colouring pen. I remember having a satchel, being made to wear a beret and being ticked off for letting my hair touch my collar. We had to eat pink semolina (a yuk milk pudding) and 'frog spawn' (a revolting, worse than yuk lumpy pudding called tapioca). It appears that Tracy Beaker agrees with me! Worst of all was having to wear a large pair of school uniform brown bloomers (knickers) over a pair of white ones! Now, that has completely blown my street cred!

Have you ever heard stories about the two World Wars? Would you like to try and find out what really happened to members of your family and what they did at that time of their lives?

By 2007 there were very few survivors of the Great War (otherwise known as The First World War) still alive, as it started over 90 years ago. However, since it became part of the National Curriculum in schools, some of the most frequent visitors to the battlefield sites are British schoolchildren of today.

I hope that by now you are beginning to want to ask questions about your family. Therefore I am going to start you off on an adventure amongst the branches of your very own family tree.

QUESTIONS TO ASK THE FAMILY

? ?? ?? ?? ?? ?

It would be great if other members of your family began to share your interest in family history. I have already suggested that you begin this hobby with a friend, but to get an adult involved could be very useful. Here are some questions that you could ask, that just might jog their memories and help them to remember and talk about the past:

- ❖ What is your earliest memory?
- ❖ Do you remember that favourite toy?
- ❖ Where did you live?
- ❖ Where did you go to school?
- ❖ What childhood diseases did you catch?
- ❖ Can you remember celebrating festivals such as Christmas?
- ❖ What was your favourite meal?
- ❖ Did you enjoy sport, and what games did you play?
- ❖ Did you have any hobbies?
- ❖ If there were any, do you remember the family pets?
- ❖ If you had a family car, can you remember what it was?
- ❖ Did you go on any holidays? If so, where?
- ❖ Did all the uncles, aunties and cousins ever come to stay? How do they fit into your family tree?
- ❖ What did your family do in the evenings?
- ❖ What sort of clothes did you wear, and were they fashionable?
- ❖ What were your favourite wireless (radio) and TV programmes?
- ❖ What magazines did you read, and did you enjoy reading books?
- ❖ Can you remember old teachers, school friends and work colleagues?
- ❖ When did you first work? What was it, and did you have to train for it?
- ❖ Can you remember your first boyfriend or girlfriend?

I am sure that you can think of lots of other questions.
I have not mentioned any of the war years here, as there would be so many things to ask. Look at pages 107-109 for some information about the Second World War.

? ?? ? ?? ? ? ?? ??

It is as well to know, before you begin, that the word 'genealogy' is just the old fashioned way of saying 'family history'.

As I have already mentioned, always start with the easiest part. If you are lucky it is possible to learn a lot about your family without going out of your front door. By saying that I do not mean sitting down in front of a computer — yet!

I have already said in the Introduction that family history can turn into a relatively expensive hobby. However I want to try and demonstrate to you that in the early days it will not, if you carefully stick to the following mostly 'free' tasks that I suggest in this chapter.

Once you have decided to make a start, begin by talking to older members of your family. Ask old family friends as well, but do remember that elderly people have this habit of getting older all the time. They could also be frail, unwell and even in some cases not want to talk about the past. However frustrating this is, you must respect this decision because there could be a very good reason and you certainly do not want to upset them. They may be willing to talk another time, but meanwhile try to resist the temptation of nagging them. When they do agree to talk with you, make sure that they do not mind notes being

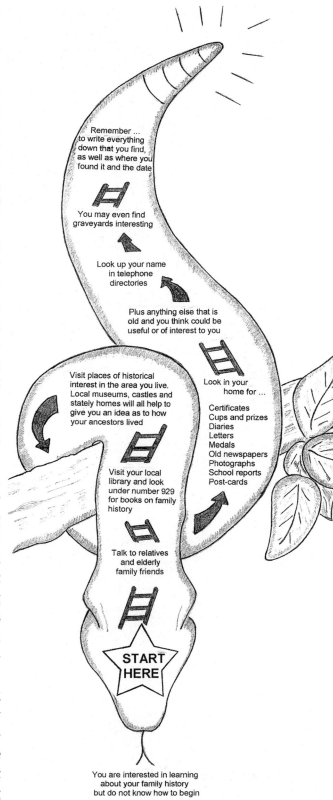

Remember ... to write everything down that you find, as well as where you found it and the date

You may even find graveyards interesting

Look up your name in telephone directories

Plus anything else that is old and you think could be useful or of interest to you

Visit places of historical interest in the area you live. Local museums, castles and stately homes will all help to give you an idea as to how your ancestors lived

Look in your home for ...

Certificates
Cups and prizes
Diaries
Letters
Medals
Old newspapers
Photographs
School reports
Post-cards

Visit your local library and look under number 929 for books on family history

Talk to relatives and elderly family friends

START HERE

You are interested in learning about your family history but do not know how to begin

taken — in fact it is better to agree everything in advance! Over the years many elderly people have not even minded being recorded onto a tape recorder, although I can sympathise with anyone not wanting to do this. A very important point is that their memories over the years are not as accurate as perhaps they once were; try not to interrupt them in full flow as you do not want to put them off. I think they can be excused quite a lot, as I am not **that** old myself but keep getting my age wrong, so how can I expect others to get it right all the time? Having said that, you would think that I am positively ancient as … yes, all right, I admit to being well over 21!

At this point I am going to mention a very common mistake that I do not want you to make. Do not fall into the trap of believing everything you hear or read — if you can, **always** check what you have learnt by going to the original source of information. I will mention this again later on, as it is very important and worthwhile advice. There must be many people around happily unaware that the information they are so proud of is completely incorrect.

Hopefully, as well as giving you plenty of information to get started, these older friends and relatives may recall family sayings, traditions or stories sometimes called folk-lore. There is a rumour that some of my family were wreckers on the south coast of Cornwall — well I have not established

that yet although I have found coastguards in the same area so I could be getting close to the truth! Wreckers were people who lured ships onto the rocky shore during the night with lanterns (so the unfortunate crew thought they were nearing a safe and friendly harbour). As the sailors drowned the wreckers stole the cargo from the doomed and sinking ship. For a modern but not nearly so evil and dramatic example we need to go no further back in time than January 2007. Because of the stormy weather, the ship *Napoli* finally ended up beached on the south Devon coast. Although no one was hurt we witnessed people looting and helping themselves to the cargo that was being washed up on the shore.

Two books for the advanced reader that deal with the subject of wreckers and wrecking are *Wreckers* by Bella Bathhurst; and *Jamaica Inn*, the very well-known and exciting novel by Daphne Du Maurier.

It does not normally take too long in family history to find what a lot of people would refer to as 'the skeleton in the cupboard'. This means something unpleasant or scandalous that is better kept as a secret to spare embarrassment. The world we live in today is full of gossip and rumour, so there is no reason to think that the lives of our ancestors were any different. Attempts were often made to keep certain stories out of the news to avoid scandal and disgrace to families. Possibly the most common reason for gossip was that of illegitimacy, which is being born without your parents being married. This would mean that instead of being called Mr. and Mrs. Bloggs, the parents would have different surnames on the birth certificate — although there are some married couples where the wife chooses not to take her husband's surname. My very old-fashioned aunt would not even acknowledge my mother's pregnancy, so imagine what her thoughts would have been if my parents had not been married! (The same aunt would not allow my father to join in the bath-time fun when I was a baby — because I was a girl!) Fortunately illegitimacy does not seem to cause too many problems nowadays, and has become an accepted way of life. Today many families are complete by the time the parents take their marriage vows.

If you are lucky, there are many - sometimes forgotten - items such as letters, medals, photographs, old newspaper articles, school reports and diaries that can still be found in your home, carefully put away in attics and desk drawers.

Some pieces of furniture, silver or china in your home could tell a story. Often on the television programme, *Antiques Roadshow,* the presenters ask if the family history of a particular object is known. The house you live in may be of great interest, as there are many very old properties still standing and each one will have a tale to tell — again, there are television programmes on this subject. The records for these properties can be found

A collection of 'treasures' and a family bible (below).

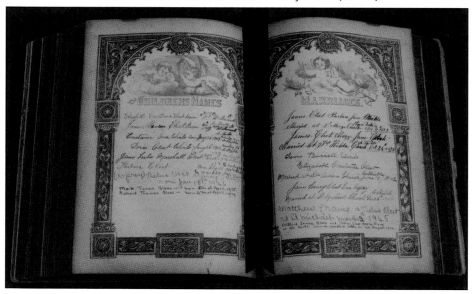

at your local County Record Office. Old maps can also be useful and very interesting.

The large family Bible was a popular place to record births, baptisms, marriages and deaths. I have been lucky, because my grandmother had a family Bible as well as lots of family photographs. These items I am certain added to this burning interest of mine to know more, although sadly the

Bible has been missing for about thirty years. These very precious pieces of history should never be allowed to leave the family, but that has happened too often. Occasionally now at such places as antique fairs, usually tucked away in a dark corner, you might come across an old photograph album. I have also seen bibles possibly a long way from their natural homes, which no one appears to want; but there must be many people who would be delighted to have the chance of having their own family copy — myself included! Do bear in mind though that sometimes the information was recorded after the event. What is written will probably be very helpful but it may not be entirely correct.

Before the invention of photography, many wealthy people relied on portrait painting. Like photographs they often portrayed the person well and illustrated strong family likenesses. Nowadays you might look at a new baby and just say, "Oh bless!" but I am sure that most people have witnessed an adult peering into a pram and saying "He **has** got his father's nose!" or "She is **just** like her grandmother!" Have you heard of the expression 'Like father, like son?' It is not always looks that are passed on; certain character features such as generosity, a desire to travel or artistic abilities can be passed down through the generations.

Occasionally the idea of a painted portrait did not always work, as in the case of a future bride of King Henry the Eighth. In 1540, when he finally met Anne of Cleves who was to be his fourth wife, he was furious that she was not as pretty as her picture. Henry called her the 'Flanders Mare' and divorced her within six months!

King Henry the Eighth and
Queen Anne of Cleves.

It is well worth a visit to your local library to see what books they have on family history. These are normally found catalogued under number 929. You may even be surprised at how helpful most of the librarians are, as they are **not** dragons in frumpy clothes telling you to be quiet all the time! — so do ask them to help you. To continue with the easiest route, a very simple thing you can do right at the start of your search, and while you are still in the library, is to look up your surname in the telephone directories. You really need to do this for all the areas in the country. Not only will this give you the exciting feeling of actually beginning, but you could find out very early on that your name is far more common in some areas of the country than others. Perhaps later on you may find out why. If you have a slightly unusual surname, you **should** find it easier to research your family's history. For example, my maiden surname before I got married was Henshelwood and most people with that name come from Scotland. I talk a little bit more about maiden surnames in Chapter 8.

Another fairly inexpensive task that you can do to help yourself get started is to visit local graveyards and cemeteries. Even if your ancestors are not buried near to your home you can get a real feeling for history whilst walking through these places. It might not do anything for your 'street cred', but you will be surprised at the amount of wildlife that is happily living amongst the dead.

While you are pottering between the gravestones you may have a younger brother or sister with you who is bored and being an absolute pain! Make the outing fun for them by making up games to play, such as looking for their first names on the headstones and working out how old the people were when they died. They could also look for unusual names.

Although not particularly funny places to be, sometimes there are some very amusing words written on gravestones — see if you can find any. However, do not forget that you are not in a playground. Please make sure that the final resting places really are left in peace by showing respect to the dead and their living relatives.

When you are in any graveyard, please be aware and very careful of any gravestones that look as if they might fall over. I certainly don't want to put you off, but there are many at the moment that could be unstable and therefore unsafe if you go too close to them.

Not so long ago many more people died when they were very young, because of lack of medical care. In some graveyards you may see a gravestone with a skull and cross bones on it — no, they were not pirates, although that is the sign of death used by pirates on their flags — this sometimes means that

Skull and cross bones on a grave in Dunfermline, Fifeshire, Scotland. Reproduced by courtesy of John Titford.

the unlucky person underneath died of the plague.

A word of warning here though — although there are a lot of small graveyards where you might easily find some of your deceased ancestors, there are many very big ones. At these you'd need to know the exact area of the grave or even the plot number, otherwise you could waste many hours just going round in circles.

While on the subject of pirates the, already mentioned, book *The Dangerous Book for Boys* shows 14 of the most famous pirate flags.

Do you know of any hobbies or collections that members of your family

Modern copy of the skull and cross bones called 'Jolly Roger' which was flown by pirate ships. In the background can be seen the cruise ship the *Black Prince*.

had? Many strange and unusual, as well as normal things, have been (and still are) collected. These range from old postcards to Pokemon cards; or butterflies, stamps, thimbles and old glass bottles to stuffed furry animals and fridge magnets. Mention any subject or item in the world and you will find that someone, somewhere has a collection! It now seems that knitting is becoming popular once more. Famous names such as Geri Halliwell, Madonna and Russell Crowe have taken up the hobby; consequently 'knit and natter' circles are springing up everywhere. Likewise the young tennis star Maria Sharapova reckons that "it's cool to collect stamps"; and because of the popular TV programme *Strictly Come Dancing*, dancing is now the fashion.

Do you enjoy looking around museums and other places of historical interest such as castles and stately homes? Here you can learn a lot about the past as well as getting 'a feel' of the local history of a particular area or place. It does not cost anything to go to many museums, which has to be a seriously good thing as far as the adults are concerned.

During your research it could be well worth your while if you can go to some family history fairs. No, I do not mean the sort of fair that has dodgem cars and shooting at targets to win a large teddy or a goldfish in a plastic bag!

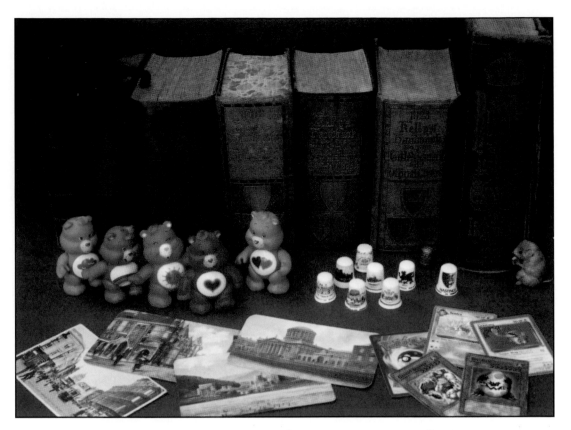

More treasures and collections.

However, you could imagine that you are on a ghost train delving into the past, as skeletons and ghosts are often considered to be the same.

These fairs are held all over the country and are advertised in libraries, local papers and on local radio. The location of the fair will normally give you an indication as to which areas in the country it will cover. Some of the bigger ones will possibly have representatives from various family history societies that are quite a long way away. I always strongly recommend joining at least one society, but I am going to talk more about that right at the end of the book. At the fairs you can browse among the bookstalls, but don't go expecting to get your favourite magazines and comics here! There are usually computer demonstrations and often other stalls that you might find interesting. Not quite the place to be seen hanging out, but I have noticed that over the years more and more young people are seen wandering around; some looking bored, but others appear to be really fascinated. If only they had books to help them! ………

To return to my statement of starting with the easiest part — if you have read and understood and then planned your first tasks, you will by now have begun your adventure into the world of family history. It is only difficult if you cannot do it, so you should have started with the known and therefore the easiest part of your journey — working towards the unknown . . . . good luck!

Important points to remember

- ❖ Family History is the modern term for genealogy.
- ❖ Talk to elderly friends and relatives as soon as possible.
- ❖ Listen carefully and write everything down.
- ❖ If using any kind of recorder — don't forget to get permission and remember the spare batteries!
- ❖ Do not always believe everything that you are told — where possible check it.
- ❖ Illegitimate means to be born to unmarried parents.
- ❖ Ask around the family for old papers, photographs etc…
- ❖ An antique is something old or old-fashioned (and often valuable) that was made a long time ago.
- ❖ Visit and make use of your local library.
- ❖ Do beware of gravestones that look as if they just might fall over.

- ❖ Do not give up if you cannot immediately find anything. The best thing to do is to go on to something else for a while.
- ❖ Everything becomes easy or easier when you know the correct procedure.

FUN AND INTERESTING WEBSITE

Try looking at some maps and put in your postcode . . .

www.multimap.com

… the expression *"If at first you don't succeed — try, try again"* is because of a spider?

The Scottish people looked to their new King for their freedom. After a particularly bloody battle Robert the Bruce took refuge in a dark cave while escaping from the English army. Robert sat and thought about how he was going to win, as at the time he felt that he had failed his people. He looked up and saw a spider climbing up its silken thread to reach the web. Again and again the spider fell, but kept on returning to try and struggle its way home. This had an amazing effect on Robert who thought that if the spider could succeed — so could he … so he picked up his sword and went on to defeat the English at the Battle of Bannockburn in 1314!

This story is told in *The Dangerous Book for Boys* by Conn and Hal Iggulden. Whether true or not it is a nice story about determination and not giving up too quickly.

A peaceful woodland cemetery in Nida, Lithuania. The very old graves are marked with wooden crosses.

The graveyard and round tower of St. Kevin's church, Glendalough, Co. Wicklow, Ireland

"In a Breckonshire Churchyard."

There are not only graveyards for human beings. The dog cemetery (right) in London is open one day a year. Reproduced by courtesy of Libby Hall, author of *Postcard Dogs*, published by Bloomsbury.

Tomb of a baby at Apethorpe near Peterborough. Photograph: Peter Watson

A grave with a view. The author's great-great-grandmother at rest over-looking the sea at Portscatho, Cornwall.

"Brusher Mills", the snake catcher of the New Forest buried at Brockenhurst.

Monument to the Mackinnon family on the island of Mull, West Scotland. It also tells us Hugh MacDonald was a schoolmaster.

G	F	J	R	P	E	D	I	G	R	E	E	N	R	K
E	D	A	M	O	U	S	E	U	Q	🌳	O	R	E	E
N	V	A	M	T	O	☺	R	A	T	S	R	E	H	L
E	🐍	O	D	I	L	T	W	R	X	R	E	D	T	C
R	N	A	L	D	L	U	A	D	O	P	T	I	O	N
A	Z	B	A	B	Y	Y	D	I	🎈HAND	N	S	P	R	U
T	S	D	R	O	C	E	R	A	A	W	I	S	B	🐭
I	N	A	U	N	T	🕸	A	N	C	E	S	T	O	R
O	E	U	H	A	N	D	N	J	Z	O	M	F	R	F
N	R	G	C	N	C	E	N	S	U	S	U	O	N	R
★	D	H	N	A	Y	R	O	T	S	I	H	S	H	I
P	L	T	A	H	A	E	D	Y	D	D	E	T	I	E
E	I	E	R	P	L	E	A	F	N	A	M	E	♥	N
T	H	R	B	R	P	R	M	U	M	M	Y	R	Q	D
S	C	H	O	O	L	T	🧸	P	A	R	E	N	T	S

WORDSEARCH

1. Family
2. Tree
3. Pedigree
4. Ancestor
5. Friends
6. Uncle
7. Records
8. Madonna
9. Baby
10. Guardian
11. Daughter
12. History
13. Aunt
14. Orphan
15. Nan
16. Parents
17. Sister
18. Foster
19. Mummy
20. Census
21. Leaf
22. Brother
23. Children
24. Daddy
25. Son
26. Generation
27. Mouse
28. Spider
29. Adoption
30. Star
31. Cousin
32, Teddy
33. Root
34. School
35. Pets
36. Name
37. Love
38. Play
39. Branch
40. Born
41. Home
42. Have a Nice Day (txt)

CHAPTER 2

Leaves on the tree

My little boy once asked me "Who had Daddy?" I replied, "Granny and Grandpa had Daddy", and this was followed by a stunned silence, a big sigh, then, "But why have we got him?" This little boy is now 27 year-old Ben!

The point that I am making here is that **everyone** has a 'natural' (real) father and a 'natural' (real) mother whether they know them or not. This is just like every living tree having leaves growing on it. 'Birth parents' is another way of referring to your natural or real parents.

Life is like a lottery, or throwing dice — we do not know what is going to happen next. When we are born, this game of chance or luck will map out our lives forever. For example do we have brothers or sisters? Are we rich, poor, clever, sporty or famous? For most of you who are none of these, I am convinced that every one of us has a talent of some sort. Occasionally it just might take a little longer to find out what it is, so do not think that you are a sad case. Hang on in there and maybe one day you'll be amazed!

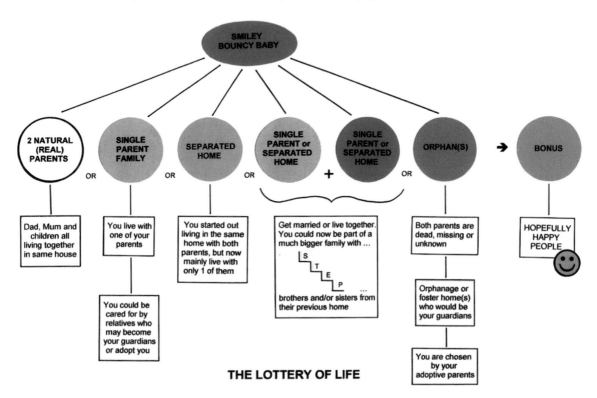

THE LOTTERY OF LIFE

Nowadays there are many people who for lots of reasons know only one of their parents, and this includes the death of a parent. A single parent family means exactly what it says — in other words, you live with either a father **or** a mother. This is sometimes called a 'separated' or a 'broken home'.

Many children live with one of their natural parents and a step-parent. As a result of this they will often have an extended family made up of step-brothers and/or step-sisters … do you recall the fairy tale of *Cinderella*?

When parents decide that they no longer want to live in the same house together, this can be very sad for everybody. This can happen to anyone as it was announced in 2003 — on Saint Valentine's Day of all days — that 'Ken and Barbie' (dolls) had split up and were getting divorced. However, in the autumn of 2005 we heard that Ken now wants Barbie back having looked carefully at his image!

Have you read any of Enid Blyton's *Adventure Series* of books, all about — Philip, Dinah, their mother and new husband Bill Cunningham and adopted orphans Jack and Lucy-Ann, with Kiki the parrot? This enlarged family continued to have the most amazing and exciting adventures together. Anne of *Anne of Green Gables* was also an orphan. Along with *Cinderella* and *Oliver Twist*, although fictional (not real), these stories and many others mirror real life situations.

Children who do not live with either of their natural parents are probably either fostered or adopted. They are loved and wanted just as much by these 'new' parents as they would be by their natural parents. After all they were especially chosen. This is certainly true in my family, because my own parents adopted my sister, Julie, when she was 5 months old. She is a doctor now and I am very proud of her although she is not my 'real' sister at all. She is my adopted sister, and 'came home' when I was 16.

Another fictional story, *Matilda* by Roald Dahl ended up with Matilda being incredibly happy. Her teacher, Miss Jennifer Honey, allowed Matilda to leave her parents and live with her instead, because she obviously loved the little girl. She had been miserable with her natural (real) parents, Mr and Mrs Wormwood, who looked upon Michael, her older brother as their favourite. I am sure that in 'real life' Miss Honey would have eventually adopted Matilda.

In her recently written book called *Nobody's Child*, the author Kate Adie takes us through many true-life cases of adoption in a very open but caring way. Although it is an adult book I am sure that the advanced teenage reader will find it both interesting and informative … and very poignant. I did.

We learnt in October 2006 that the pop star Madonna adopted a young boy called David from Malawi. In 2007 the actress Angelina Jolie adopted a

Marilyn Monroe

3 year old Vietnamese boy. He joins Maddox from Cambodia, Zahara from Ethiopia and Shiloh. Angelina and Brad Pitt are the natural (real) parents of Shiloh Nouvel who was born in Namibia.

The famous film star Marilyn Monroe had a very unhappy childhood and was brought up in several orphanages and foster homes. If you have never heard of her I am sure that you will know of an adult who has — especially the dads, granddads and uncles!

An orphan is a child whose parents have died or are missing, and an orphanage is a place where orphans and abandoned children are looked after. Foster homes are where people (known as foster parents) temporarily care for children along with their own families and in their own homes. Some children are brought up and cared for by relatives such as grandparents. Whatever the situation, the person or people who do the caring and looking after become the child's 'guardians'.

Sadly, since Boxing Day 2004 we have been hearing about orphanages in the areas hit by the tsunami. An earthquake in the Indian Ocean caused a massive wave which drowned many thousands of people. This dreadful, but natural disaster was responsible for making thousands of children into homeless orphans.

Those of you who have read the books will remember that Harry Potter was made an orphan after Lord Voldemort murdered his parents. He lived for a while with his rather unpleasant Uncle Vernon, Aunt Petunia and their fat, "pig in a wig" son Dudley. The Dursleys had not adopted Harry, so they would have been either his guardians or foster parents if they had been real people in the real world. Those of you who are adopted, fostered or have guardians could have difficulties in finding out about your natural (real) parents. If your questions cannot be answered, you may have to go to special records to continue your journey, but I hope that this will not easily put you off.

For the rest of you, to keep things as simple as possible, for the moment I am going to assume that you live with, or know at least one of your parents.

I am hoping that by now you will have found out enough information to be able to start drawing up your very own Family Tree. This is the exciting bit when the jigsaw puzzle actually begins to take shape but do **not** worry if you cannot fill in many of the names.

There are several ways of drawing a family tree, but you must always begin at the beginning and start with yourself. Imagine yourself as the star on the tree so the first name that you write down will be your own. The next 2 names up are those of your parents and the top 4 will be the names of your 4 grandparents. In other words you are working backwards and this is shown in the illustration below.

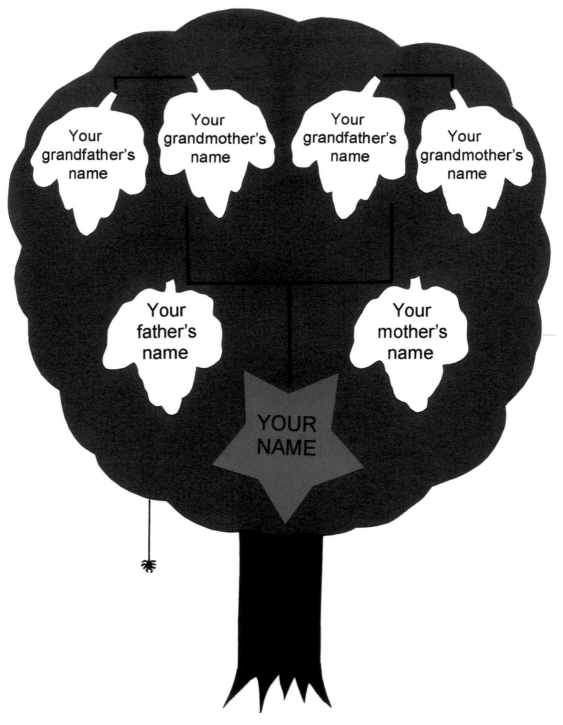

If you know any details of your 8 great-grandparents you can now add another line to the top of your tree and put in their names.

Have you noticed that the name on the left hand side of each set of parents is the male name? It is usual to put the male names first.

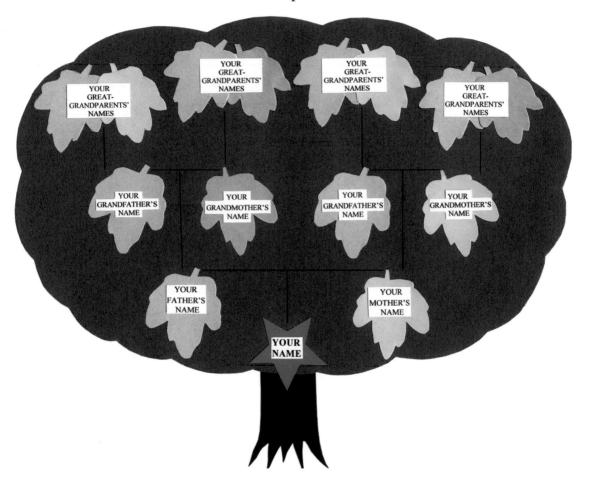

As you are now familiar with the words family tree, another word meaning the same thing is pedigree, which means a list of ancestors.

Have you heard people talk about pedigree dogs? There are also many other different types of pedigree animals. Do you remember hearing, or reading about, some of the valuable pedigree farm animals that were at risk of having to be destroyed during the Foot and Mouth Disease out-breaks? A lot were, but luckily we heard of many that were saved including Phoenix the white calf who is now a mum herself. Of course we do not forget here either all the other non-pedigree animals that had to be put to sleep. A story called *Out of the Ashes* by Michael Morpurgo is based on true events of the 2001 Foot and Mouth Disease. The Book is dedicated to all the farmers and farming communities who suffered from the out-breaks.

All these pedigree animals are far more expensive than the common farm-yard cow or mongrel dog (mongrel means mixed breed or non-pedigree). This is because their parents are the same as themselves, for example a pedigree poodle dog meeting and mating with another pedigree poodle will produce pedigree poodle puppies and their pedigree means that their ancestry can be recorded in a similar way to ours. In other words, we know who their parents, grandparents and great-grandparents were. Our pedigree dog, a whippet called Geordie who was quite expensive, has a pedigree (family tree) going back for 5 generations and we know the names of all his 62 whippet ancestors — that includes his great-great-great-grandparents! Because dogs do not live nearly as long as us human beings, and breed when young, we are only talking of going back something like 20 years.

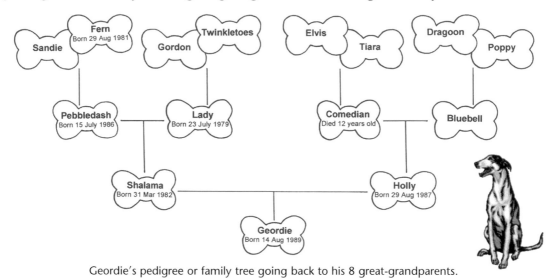

Geordie's pedigree or family tree going back to his 8 great-grandparents.

However, a father poodle and a mother cocker spaniel will produce mongrel puppies instead of pedigree puppies. These are now fashionably called 'cockerpoos'! Pug and beagle 'parents' will produce a 'puggle', dachshund and corgi parents produce a 'dorgi' and a Labrador and a poodle will have — yes! — a labradoodle.

Our other dog, Daisy, was not expensive and is a loopy, but very loveable mongrel lurcher with hilarious ears but no pedigree. We do know who her mother is, but her father is unknown. If she was a human being instead of a dog we could say that she is illegitimate.

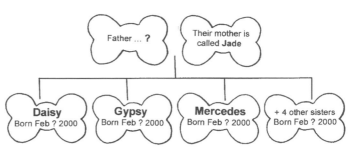

Daisy's non pedigree. This is all we know of her family tree.

38

I have included the next illustration, to show you that beside the names there are some extra letters that are called abbreviations. It will now help you to know what these mean . . .

bn — born   m — married   d — died

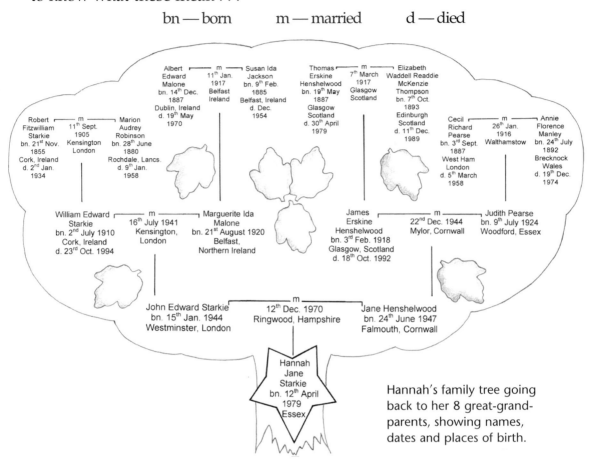

Albert Edward Malone
bn. 14ᵗʰ Dec. 1887
Dublin, Ireland
d. 19ᵗʰ May 1970

— m —
11ᵗʰ Jan. 1917
Belfast Ireland

Susan Ida Jackson
bn. 9ᵗʰ Feb. 1885
Belfast, Ireland
d. Dec. 1954

Thomas Erskine Henshelwood
bn. 19ᵗʰ May 1887
Glasgow Scotland
d. 30ᵗʰ April 1979

— m —
7ᵗʰ March 1917
Glasgow Scotland

Elizabeth Waddell Readdie McKenzie Thompson
bn. 7ᵗʰ Oct. 1893
Edinburgh Scotland
d. 11ᵗʰ Dec. 1989

Robert Fitzwilliam Starkie
bn. 21ˢᵗ Nov. 1855
Cork, Ireland
d. 2ⁿᵈ Jan. 1934

— m —
11ᵗʰ Sept. 1905
Kensington London

Marion Audrey Robinson
bn. 28ᵗʰ June 1880
Rochdale, Lancs.
d. 9ᵗʰ Jan. 1958

Cecil Richard Pearse
bn. 3ʳᵈ Sept. 1887
West Ham London
d. 5ᵗʰ March 1958

— m —
26ᵗʰ Jan. 1916
Walthamstow

Annie Florence Manley
bn. 24ᵗʰ July 1892
Brecknock Wales
d. 19ᵗʰ Dec. 1974

William Edward Starkie
bn. 2ⁿᵈ July 1910
Cork, Ireland
d. 23ʳᵈ Oct. 1994

— m —
16ᵗʰ July 1941
Kensington, London

Marguerite Ida Malone
bn. 21ˢᵗ August 1920
Belfast, Northern Ireland

James Erskine Henshelwood
bn. 3ʳᵈ Feb. 1918
Glasgow, Scotland
d. 18ᵗʰ Oct. 1992

— m —
22ⁿᵈ Dec. 1944
Mylor, Cornwall

Judith Pearse
bn. 9ᵗʰ July 1924
Woodford, Essex

John Edward Starkie
bn. 15ᵗʰ Jan. 1944
Westminster, London

— m —
12ᵗʰ Dec. 1970
Ringwood, Hampshire

Jane Henshelwood
bn. 24ᵗʰ June 1947
Falmouth, Cornwall

Hannah Jane Starkie
bn. 12ᵗʰ April 1979
Essex

Hannah's family tree going back to her 8 great-grandparents, showing names, dates and places of birth.

There are two things to notice in the above illustration, other than there being a lot more information on it. First of all, you should begin to see a pattern forming. Have you spotted that the number of ancestors double each time you go back another line — or generation? This is shown in the simple diagram. Secondly, you can see that sometimes certain names were often passed down through the generations. The names Edward, Erskine, Ida, Jane and William all feature twice with different people. Erskine is a Scottish clan name.

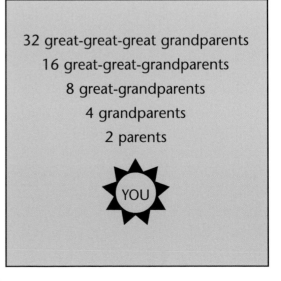

32 great-great-great grandparents

16 great-great-grandparents

8 great-grandparents

4 grandparents

2 parents

YOU

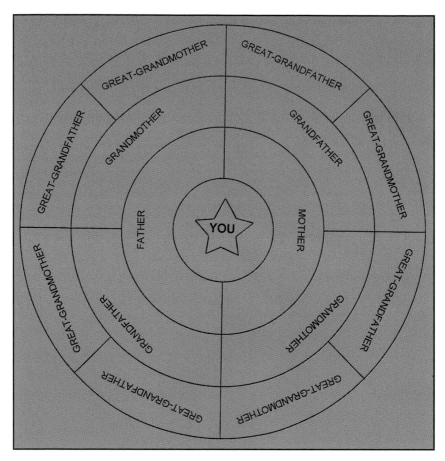

You can also lay out your family tree on a circular chart like this.

Another 'fun' way to lay out your family tree is to use a circular chart as shown in the illustration above.

You have now learnt how to lay out your family tree and have actually started to put some names on it. I hope that you have become even more curious to know about your family and will want to search for all those missing pieces. 'Putting flesh on the bones' is another way of saying that you want to find out other information, for example details of siblings (another word for brothers and sisters), and where your ancestors lived and went to school. Knowledge of social history — this is the way we used to live — is another part of your family's history; it will have played a very important part in your past and could give you some clues to help with your puzzle.

Something to keep at the back of your mind is the practice of having 'unofficial relations'. These could just be friends or neighbours of your parents that you have been brought up to call 'Uncle' or 'Auntie', regardless of the fact that they are not really related to you at all. Nevertheless they will remain a large part of your life and may be able to help you to fill in some of the missing pieces.

Important points to remember

- ❖ Every baby born has a natural (real) father and a natural (real) mother.

- ❖ Being part of a single parent family is living with either a father or a mother.

- ❖ A step-parent — is the new husband or partner of a child's natural mother, or the new wife or partner of a child's natural father.

- ❖ To foster — is to bring up and temporarily care for a child that is not your own natural child.

- ❖ Adoption is to choose a child and legally become his or her new parents.

- ❖ An orphan is a child whose parents are missing, unknown or no longer alive.

- ❖ A guardian is someone who is legally responsible for caring for a child.

- ❖ When drawing your family tree always start with yourself.

- ❖ A pedigree is a 'list' of ancestors and so another word for family tree.

- ❖ Sibling is another word for a brother or sister.

- ❖ Spouse is another word for a husband or a wife.

FUN AND INTERESTING WEBSITES

Click on 'history for kids' on the BBC's interesting website
www.bbc.co.uk/history

Children in Care 1881-1918 - Hidden Lives Revealed
www.hiddenlives.org.uk

Beamish the North of England Open Air Museum
www.beamish.org.uk

The Iron Gorge Museums in Shropshire
www.ironbridge.org.uk

Can you match these clothes with the correct description?

1. liberty bodice
2. handkerchief
3. petticoat
4. plus fours/breeches
5. combinations
6. tunic
7. corset
8. tam-o'shanter
9. mackintosh
10. pinafore

a. used for blowing your nose - like a tissue
b. shapeless, sleeveless short dress worn by schoolgirls
c. a raincoat made of a rubbery/waterproof material
d. tight-fitting items of women's underwear, sometimes stiffened with strips of bone or metal called 'stays'. Also called a teddy
e. a Scottish hat very like the French beret but with a pompom
f. a thin skirt worn by women under clothes. Can also be called a shift, slip or chemise
g. a protective cover or apron worn over clothes
h. all-in-one underwear
i. a woman's thick vest with rubber buttons - a little bit like a camisole
j. trousers that only go down to the knees

These bridesmaids and page-boys don't look terribly happy or pleased. Photograph taken in Oxford in 1928. Turn to Chapter 4 for more wedding fashions.

DID YOU KNOW ... how to tell the age of a person?

In Victorian times a gentleman would hand this table to a young lady, and ask her to tell him in which column or columns her age is contained. He would then add together the numbers at the top of the columns in which her age was to be found – and would then know her secret! For example, suppose her age is 18, you will find that number in the 2nd and 5th columns – add together the top numbers of these two columns.

1	2	4	8	16	32
3	3	5	9	17	33
5	6	6	10	18	34
7	7	7	11	19	35
9	10	12	12	20	36
11	11	13	13	21	37
13	14	14	14	22	38
15	15	15	15	23	39
17	18	20	24	24	40
19	19	21	25	25	41
21	22	22	26	26	42
23	23	23	27	27	43
25	26	28	28	28	44
27	27	29	29	29	45
29	30	30	30	30	46
31	31	31	31	31	47
33	34	36	40	48	48
35	35	37	41	49	49
37	38	38	42	50	50
39	39	39	43	51	51
41	42	44	44	52	52
43	43	45	45	53	53
45	46	46	46	54	54
47	47	47	47	55	55
49	50	52	56	56	56
51	51	53	57	57	57
53	54	54	58	58	58
55	55	55	59	59	59
57	58	60	60	60	60
59	59	61	61	61	61
61	62	62	62	62	62
63	63	63	63	63	63

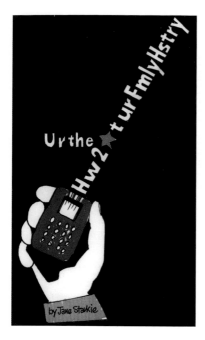

Ur the ★ 2 t ur Fmly Hstry

Hw 2 ★ t ur Fmly Hstry

by Jane Starkie

CHAPTER 3

B4UBGN

Get connected

Before you begin to spend any money on birth, marriage or death certificates, now is the time to give yourself a large dollop of street cred and give it a whirl on the computer.

It was my husband John who pointed out that the two things that many people are afraid of are spiders and mice. When you sit gazing at your computer screen you are surrounded by world-wide webs and a mouse.

Please remember **always** to check the original records when and where possible. I mention how important this is in Chapter 1. The computer cannot be blamed if the information put into it at the beginning was incorrect. Although as more and more sites are offering images of scanned-in documents, the problem of finding wrongly-transcribed information is getting less. However, if you come across the name of someone that you have been looking for, hang fire before you do somersaults of joy like a footballer. Remember that as you started with yourself as the *star*, so you must be able to prove that the name you have found is in fact an ancestor of yours.

FrEE access TO THE WEb

More information is added to the internet all the time. New websites are being created every day; others are either being updated or discontinued, so whatever information I give you could be out-of-date very soon.

I am also certain that you will know far more than I do about computers, as you will have been brought up with them. Having said that, I know many 'silver surfers' (grans and grand-dads) who are continually 'surfing the net'.

My brain tells me that surfing was something that I used to do in the sea when I was much younger, 'grazing' was what our cows did to produce milk on my parents' farm in Cornwall and to 'boot up' meant to put on your wellies. I also recall having 'Spam' sandwiches for picnics on the beach. 'Spam' was a post-war reconstituted meat product (**S**eparately **P**acked **A**merican **M**eat), which I understand the unwanted junk emails of today are named after.

Personally I find it far more exciting to discover something that is written in a book or document rather than seeing it on a screen in front of me. I have great satisfaction in knowing that I had far more to do with the actual detective work of searching and finding, instead of the computer doing most of it for me. Besides, you cannot always take the computer to bed with you. A friend of mine used a torch to read under the duvet, so that she wouldn't wake her husband up — can you imagine the hassle involved if she had decided to do a few spreadsheets on the PC? There is no doubt though, that computer skills are far faster than the human brain and for many tasks the computer will be extremely valuable. Having

Computers have become much smaller. This one was at King's College, London, in 1968.

said that, you still have to be the detective when using a computer: you have to work out which sites to visit and what to search for.

Meanwhile you must ask yourself, "How can I use the computer to trace my family tree?"

I'm sure that the first thing that you will think of is the internet. It is true to say that there are lots of websites that are very useful; and it is now actually possible to trace ancestors on the internet. As I write this, Google, www.google.com is possibly the best and fastest search engine. Type in words such as 'family tree', 'ancestors' or 'genealogy' and see what you get as you scroll through.

Another use of computers for family history is that you may be able to contact fellow researchers by email.

A friend, when giving talks on family history, gives his audience what he thinks to be the 10 most important websites. I am going to give 10 here that take into consideration the low costs (if any) involved and, the reliability of the sites, but there are also other sites mentioned in the next two chapters. Some of the names do sound rather like pop groups ☺ but I assure you they are not ☹!

The following ten sites are in no particular order of preference …

1. GENUKI: www.genuki.org.uk
This website is probably the best place to start looking for your ancestors in the UK and Ireland. There is plenty of information with links to every part of the British Isles. You can search by topic, such as churchyards, or by place — try your home-town.

2. Cyndi's List: www.cyndislist.com
Goes well with GENUKI and, is especially useful for places outside the British Isles.

3. FamilySearch: www.familysearch.org
Another huge site which is compiled by The Church of Jesus Christ of Latter Day Saints (also known as the LDS Church or the Mormons). It has some useful tips for your research but it is best for records before 1900.

This website also includes free access to transcriptions of the 1881 Census and some parish records.

'Granite Mountain Records Vault' in the mountains near Salt Lake City, Utah, USA, where records are stored.

4. The Federation of Family History Societies (FFHS): www.ffhs.org.uk
This is the Federation of Family History Societies' website. A useful site, to enable you to find out which society covers the particular area that you are interested in. It will also bring you some of the latest news from the UK family history world.

CWG	
Commonwealth War Graves Commiss	

Casualty Details

Name:	PEARSE, FRANK ARTHUR
Initials:	F A
Nationality:	United Kingdom
Rank:	Second Lieutenant
Regiment/Service:	Somerset Light Infantry
Unit Text:	1st Bn.
Age:	24
Date of Death:	02/07/1916
Additional information:	Son of Henry Charles and Clara Pearse, of 14, Eaton Place, Brighton.
Casualty Type:	Commonwealth War Dead
Grave/Memorial Reference:	Pier and Face 2 A.
Memorial:	**THIEPVAL MEMORIAL**

Search Page | Certificate

Home | Site Map | Contact Us | Useful Links | Debt of Honour | Privacy Policy | Terms and Conditions | Cre

The website of the Commonwealth War Graves Commission.

5. Commonwealth War Graves Commission: www.cwgc.org
Contains details of the armed forces who died in action during the two world wars and gives locations of their graves. It also includes some civilians that were killed by enemy action.

6. GOONS: www.one-name.org
Find out whether anyone else has already traced the names or families that you are looking for. This is the website of the Guild of One-Name Studies.

7. Scotland: www.scotlandspeople.gov.uk is the official government website.

8. Ireland: www.nationalarchives.ie
Under 'genealogy' you will find links to family history sites.

9. **UK BMD:** www.ukbmd.org.uk
Contains links to many of the on-line registrars' indexes of births, marriages and deaths for England, Northern Ireland, Scotland and Wales.

10. **Ancestry**: www.ancestry.co.uk
Although this site requires payment, because it is such a fast growing and popular site, I feel that it cannot be left out.

The second point is that there are loads of CDs available containing all sorts of family history information. However I really do not think you need to be buying anything like this yet. I am not even going to mention any particular ones here, as I would far rather that you get to know a lot more about the subject of family history first.

Finally, you can use a family history program on your computer. These are designed to help you to record all your information in a logical sequence. Two of the better-known ones are called *Family Tree Maker* and *Family Historian*. Once you have keyed in the information, they can automatically draw family trees and produce printed family record sheets. Photos can also be scanned into the computer to enable you to produce family trees with family pictures. These programs are not free; to give you an idea of the cost have a browse on the internet.

There are also completely free family history freeware programs available, which you can download and use. Two examples are *Legacy* (which can be downloaded from www.legacyfamilytree.com) and, *Heredis* (www.myheredis.com).

Whilst I am still on computers I cannot leave out *Friends Reunited*, which I'm sure many of you will have discovered already. This started a few years ago mainly for long-lost school and college friends to find each other. It seems to be a very popular website, with a member of the Royal Family and

'Little Miss Muffet'
This picture was painted by Arthur Rackham for Queen Mary's Doll's House at Windsor Castle. It measures 3.8cm x 2.5 cm.

several well-known celebrities as members. Some people have sadly used it to say some rather unkind things about their teachers. Most of them could be true of course, but this is not really the place to tell those juicy, gossipy tales!

Genes Connected is a newer website which concentrates on family history. It is proving to be very popular with people that are trying to find lost relations. Imagine suddenly getting a letter or an email from a relative that you never knew you even had. Both www.friendsreunited.co.uk and www.genesconnected.co.uk sites are free to register with, and you can obtain a lot of information before you have to part with any money.

Although nothing to do with computers, I feel that now is the time to mention yet another place to look that might contain something of interest to you. If you have Teletext on your TV, go to Channel Four. On the 'menu' you should find a Family Tree section and more recently 'Lost Touch' (which is for people who were in the armed forces). It is possible that an ancestor who fought in the Second World War could be named here. I am not going to give actual page numbers because they are constantly changing. The information is not in alphabetical order; however, it is a completely free service.

Important points to remember

- ❖ Please remember to ask permission before using the internet.
- ❖ Don't forget that the information you find on the internet will need careful checking whenever possible.
- ❖ A census in family history means a count (with names) of people. For more on censuses please go to Chapter 5.
- ❖ Parish records are church records, and for more details please go to page 67.
- ❖ Immigration is the travelling of people from one country to another to live there.
- ❖ The armed forces of a country include the army, navy and air force.

THINGS THAT YOUR GREAT-GRANDMOTHER MIGHT NEVER HAVE DONE . . . when young

* Used a mobile phone or sent a txt msg
* Used a computer, sent an email or 'surfed the net' using such things as Facebook and Blogs
* Eaten a Big Mac, because she would have thought it was a large raincoat! In 1974 the first McDonalds opened in London
* Used soft loo paper or popped to the loo along the corridor. Many 'privies' were outside in the yard or garden
* Worn designer clothes, replica sports' kits, tights, 'Bling', trainers or green wellies. She and her friends would not have been 'hoodies' and would have thought WAGs were witty people
* Eaten an Indian or Chinese takeaway … or had a pizza delivered
* Shopped until she had dropped with a credit card
* Gone in the car to do a supermarket shop, or to the pub for some grub. To her a 4X4 and a BLT could have been mathematical sums or codes
* Watched TV, DVD, played on a PlayStation or owned an iPod
* Put a disposable nappy on the baby's bottom
* Eaten ready-made meals, junk food or cooked frozen food
* Walked her labradoodle (yes, honest! It's a cross between a labrador and a poodle), or a cockerpoo (a cross between a cocker spaniel and a poodle)
* Travelled on a plane, on a motorway or crossed the Channel by car
* Used a Ladyshave, hair straighteners, hair spray or gel
* Walked down Main Street at a Disney theme park; or even gone on an 'away day' to Alton Towers or the London Eye
* Read *Harry Potter*, bounced on **a** bouncy castle, been to a 'sleep-over' or gone clubbing; and she would have probably never used a swear word
* Worn a thong, held an Ann Summers Party or heard of the expression 'All fur coat and no knickers'
* Visited garden centres, assembled a 'flat-pack' or held a coffee morning
* Stayed alive, if in desperate need of antibiotics such as penicillin
* 'Moved in' with her boyfriend or taken the pill. As for showing off her tummy … especially when pregnant, WELL words would have failed her!

A lot of the above had not been invented in her time, others were very new and not yet easily available except possibly to rich people.

Your great-grandmother would not have sat around 'chilling out', nor would she have heard of the words — stressed out. Unless people were wealthy, generally there was always something to do such as sewing, mending, knitting or darning socks. Doing the housework such as scrubbing the front doorstep and 'blacking' the stove as well as providing home-made meals would have made her the dutiful housewife. In many cases she would have struggled to just keep going.

SQUARE SNAKE PUZZLE

Starting with number 1 find the correct answer to the clues.

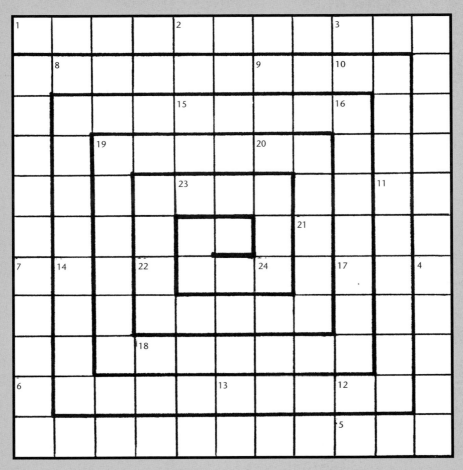

1. A relative
2. Another word for 'return' on keyboard
3. People connected by blood marriage
4. Brother or sister
5. Time between the birth of parents and children
6. Given at birth
7. Tape, like a rubber band
8. A count of people
9. Cry
10. These certificates are red
11. School subject
12. Spiritual exercise
13. Person you are descended from
14. Taken each school morning
15. Parts of a tree underground
16. Take all your clothes off
17. Family tree
18. . . . to be married
19. These certificates are black
20. Hurt
21. These certificates are green
22. A girl's name
23. Room at the top of a house
24. See you later (txt)

CHAPTER 4

Hatched, matched and despatched

You have by now gathered as much information as you can from talking to the elderly relatives and family friends, and may have had a bit of fun surfing the net.

I hope that you've been lucky and have found all sorts of interesting bits and pieces that will help you with your puzzle, as well as having lots of ideas. Having made a start at filling in your family tree (see diagram on page 36), you have made plenty of careful notes — haven't you? Every time you discover something, it is very important to write down the date and exactly where you found it — and that means the exact book or record as well as the place. Much later this may help to jog your memory as well as saving yourself a lot of time, because sometimes you may need to check the details again. It is so easy to say to yourself that of course you will remember — but I bet you don't!

'Marriage by Registrar' by W. Dendy Sadler.

Reproduced by courtesy of Thomas Ross Ltd. Copyright © The Thomas Ross Collection

'Hatched, Matched and Despatched' is the nickname given to the part of newspapers that print information of recent births, marriages and deaths.

Details of births, marriages and deaths, along with additional information, are on certificates that can be fairly easily obtained (but you have to find them first), and will help you on your journey into the past. If you haven't spent much money yet, now is the time that you will start as these certificates are not free. Ordering the wrong one will cost you, so it is important to be as sure as possible that you have found the right person. Perhaps adults that share an interest in your new hobby would be willing to help out with the expense, especially if it is their family that you are researching. The current price for a certificate is £7.

Birth certificate - Office for National Statistics - © Crown copyright. Reproduced with the permission of the Controller of HMSO and Queen's Printer for Scotland.

No. (Number)	When and where born	Name if any	Sex (Boy or girl)	Name and surname of father	Name, surname and maiden surname of mother	Occupation of father	Signature, description and residence of informant	When registered	Signature of registrar	Name entered after registration

Information given on a birth certificate for England and Wales.

You might have seen a birth, marriage or death certificate, so you will recognise the last illustration, which records the birth of my grandmother. Everybody should have a birth certificate, hopefully kept in a safe place at home. You never know when you will need it; applying for a passport is one instance when it will have to be shown.

By now you will have discovered that lots of 'pieces' of your family puzzle are missing. You will probably now need to get some certificates to take you further back in time.

Bishop's Stortford Register Office.

If you are able, it is now time to take your ancestor hunt to your local register office or General Register Office. These are the places to obtain birth, marriage and death certificates (collectively called civil registration, - see page 66 for further information). This is when you really begin to turn 'detective' because you will need to work out carefully what to do first.

To trace the correct certificate for a particular person, the more details and clues that you have the better. As already mentioned, a wrong certificate will be an expensive mistake.

First of all you will need to find the register office for the area where your ancestors lived - either under 'Registration of Births, Marriages & Deaths' in the local telephone directory, or through the UK BMD website (www.ukbmd.org.uk/genuki/reg/regoff.html). Do not just turn up on their doorstep as they could be at lunch or conducting a wedding ceremony. Mondays are normally busy days after the weekend, so it is best to avoid them. To prevent disappointment and a waste of your time, it is advisable to ring to find out the opening times and book an appointment. You cannot normally personally search the indexes. You can obtain certificates from other register offices in the country either by post or visiting them yourself, but I stress

Shelves at a Register Office showing the registers.

again that they only keep the local records of their particular area.

The other register offices from which you can obtain birth, marriage and death certificates are the General Register Offices (GROs). The GRO for England and Wales is in Southport, near Liverpool. There the records date back to July 1837. They will send you certificates by post if you can give them enough information.

Many large libraries have copies of the complete GRO civil registration indexes from 1837 on microfiche (see important points to remember at the end of this chapter). These are available to look at, once again proving what an excellent service the libraries provide. You cannot purchase certificates in libraries, but you can make notes of all the details and, as mentioned above, then apply to the GRO in Southport by post or through their website at www.gro.gov.uk (on-line ordering is now possible).

To return to the computer, you can also view most of the GRO indexes at pay-per-view websites like www.findmypast.com or www.ancestry.com. This could end up being both costly and time-consuming especially if you are looking for a fairly common name. If you are lucky, then your local library will let you use these sites for free, if they have a subscription. The more unusual the name, the easier the task should be.

Although www.FreeBMD.org.uk doesn't have all the GRO indexes yet, it is free to use. A lot of local register offices have started to put their indexes on-line for free as well - you can find them through www.ukbmd.org.uk.

There are other GROs in Belfast (for certificates in Northern Ireland),

HATCHED, MATCHED . . .

It is now becoming popular to have the civil ceremony followed by a church blessing, like Prince Charles and Camilla, Duchess of Cornwall. Julie (my sister) and Richard got married at the Register Office in the morning in February 2007. This legal ceremony, with no guests and casual clothes, was followed in the afternoon with all the formality of the Church Blessing.

Benjamin being weighed.

Below: Julie and Richard, February 2007.

Today many families are complete by the time the parents take their marriage vows. Edward and Natasha in August 2007 with baby Niamh.
Photograph David Court www.courtoncamera.co.uk

Above left: Mike and Jo after their village wedding in 2003.

Above right: Neil and Louise Macleod were married in July 2007.

. . . and DESPATCHED

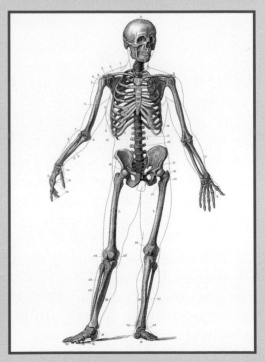

INTERESTING WEBSITE
Find a grave at
www.findagrave.com

Dublin (the Republic of Ireland) and Edinburgh (Scotland). These have the records just for their own countries, but unlike Southport you can normally visit them to search in person.

It is wonderful if you happen to live close to one of these places, but not at all helpful if you live hundreds of miles away. However, you can apply for certificates by post, and probably by now most places will enable you to print off certificate application forms from their websites. Quite often, there are day trips at very reasonable prices organised by local family history societies. How about getting an older friend or relative to make the first trip for you, suss the whole thing out and apply for any certificates while you spend the day at school! Before you make too many plans, it is advisable to make sure that the GRO is open as usual on the day of the proposed visit.

I am not going into any more details of the information recorded on the different certificates or how to go about obtaining them. There are usually free leaflets telling you what to do, and you can always ask for help. You'll find that, like the libraries, the staff are very helpful and know what they are talking about.

It is quite an experience when you suddenly discover someone that you have been trying to find for ages. The name seems to jump out at you from the many lists that you will see, and you want to jump up and shout out "Yesssss!" That is how I felt the first time and even now, 39 years later, it can be a wonderful 'historical moment'.

Occasionally you might not be able to find what you're looking for, despite all the efforts of playing the detective. Since I started all those years ago I have been looking for an ancestor who would have been born about 1864. I confidently expected to find her immediately with no such luck, although I feel sure that I'll track her down one day. Meanwhile, it is very frustrating because I have quite a few photographs of her; I even have a ring and a string of pearls that once belonged to her (see illustration on page 59).

When looking through the indexes and you cannot find the entry that you expect to, you need to be aware that the spelling of names can vary considerably. Also, the spelling of names could sometimes have been written down incorrectly. This can make your search more complicated, as you might need to think of other ways of spelling the name that you are looking for. For example our surname is Starkie, but there are many who have the alternative surname of Starkey. Over the years we have had letters addressed to us as Mr. and Mrs. **S**par**k**ie, **S**par**k**le, Star**k**le, Sta**lk**ey, St**o**rkie, St**r**a**k**ey and Sta**lin**!

The further you go back in time, you will find that more and more people were illiterate — this means that they couldn't read or write. When an illiterate person needed to sign a certificate or document they would put an **X,** and then someone else would sign for them. No, don't go thinking that they were being friendly and putting a kiss as a sign of affection!

Photograph showing some Starkie treasures. Can you spot the ring on the mouse's head?

Marriages used to take place in churches, chapels or register offices. Since 1995, people have been getting married in certain stately homes, hotels and even exotic beaches on Mediterranean or Caribbean Islands. All these places however, have to obtain a licence to allow the civil ceremony to take place. This is conducted by the local registrar. Skibo Castle in Scotland is becoming a fashionable place for the rich and famous to get married. Could this be because Madonna chose to get married there?

Similarly, instead of the traditional baptism (christening) many parents are now choosing to have civil 'naming ceremonies' for their children.

As already mentioned, the government is reviewing civil registration. Watch this space. In the future it may even be possible to get married in all sorts of places including your own home.

A long, long time ago in our part of the world, there were many 'arranged' marriages. This often happened within royal, aristocratic and wealthy families, either to improve relations

Left: Paul and Sheila signing the register at their Register Office Ceremony.

Right: Alan and Karen signing the marriage register on February 15th 2003, the day after Saint Valentine's Day.

Below: Dean, from Malta, and Kathy just married at the Catholic Cathedral, Portsmouth.

Above: Ted and Tania, just married on a beach in Mexico.

The marriage of Alix and Shaun, On the left is the bride (Alix) with her mum Paula.

between countries or because the kings were so desperate to produce sons to follow them. Do you remember the story of Henry the Eighth and Anne of Cleves that I talked about in Chapter 1? They met for the first time when she came to England for their wedding. There was often very little love or affection in these marriages; it was just convenient for parents or others who could see many advantages including improving their lifestyle. In many cases the child bride and bridegroom did not even know each other, nor had they met until the actual wedding day. They did not always like what they saw when they came face to face at the altar. Can you imagine your parents telling you one day that you are going to marry some unknown spotty nerd, a fat and frumpy daughter of a lord or a skanky old geezer (possibly known to you as 'Swamp donkeys') from far away just because it will make them rich!

Some were so desperate to produce a son and heir; that it was rumoured in 1688 that a baby boy was smuggled into the bed of Mary of Modena, the Queen-wife of King James the Second . . . in a warming pan.

Conversely in the world today arranged marriages are still celebrated in some countries. It is fairly common in the Asian communities here in the United Kingdom. To many people nowadays this would seem to be a strange custom but to others it is perfectly normal. Let's face it, there are plenty of couples who do not get it right even when they choose their own partner, so having it all decided for you must save a great deal of hassle.

Despite the fact that we sometimes get to hear about unhappy marriages; the owners of my village shop know a happily married couple, with two

Indu and Pathmanathan celebrating their arranged wedding in a Hindu temple. You can see that Indu changes into a new sari (from her husband) during the ceremony.

62

children. They had an arranged marriage, which was a Hindu wedding ceremony. Hinduism is a religion predominantly in India. I understand that before everything is finally arranged, the family histories of the bride and groom are studied carefully. Their horoscopes are also carefully examined.

An interesting book that I ordered from the children's library explains very well the differences between the main religions of the World. As well as describing some of their religious customs, it also describes the way these religions celebrate births and marriages, and deal with death. The book is called *What I Believe* and is written by Alan Brown and Andrew Langley.

Important points to remember

❖ Check before you travel that the register office, or anywhere else that you are planning to visit, is open on the day you have arranged. Many of them now have their own websites giving such information as opening times.

❖ It would also be worth checking that there is no age restriction at your planned destination. Not all record offices welcome young people. However, I am pleased to say that more are finally coming round to being young person friendly, and are actively seeking ways of attracting you to visit them.

❖ Civil registration is the recording of the birth, marriage and death of every man, woman and child.

❖ An index is the alphabetical listing of names **with the surname usually written first**.

❖ Microfiche, also called fiche, is a sheet of film a bit like a photographic negative, usually measuring 10 by 15 centimetres. Each sheet of film contains masses of information. To view, it is inserted into a machine called a microfiche reader (not to be confused with a microfilm reader), which acts like a magnifying glass and enlarges the images for easier reading.

❖ Remember that names could have been spelt differently or incorrectly.

❖ 'Illiterate' means a person who cannot read or write.

❖ A document is another name for an official piece of paper such as a letter, record or report.

❖ It would be a good idea to make a note if you do not find anything at all. This may save you from wasting time by looking again at a later date.

❖ Addresses of some of the places mentioned in this chapter are at the end of the book.

❖ Non-religious naming ceremonies are becoming popular as an alternative to the religious baptism or christening.

❖ If you cannot find an entry, it is always worth searching the years before and after the expected event.

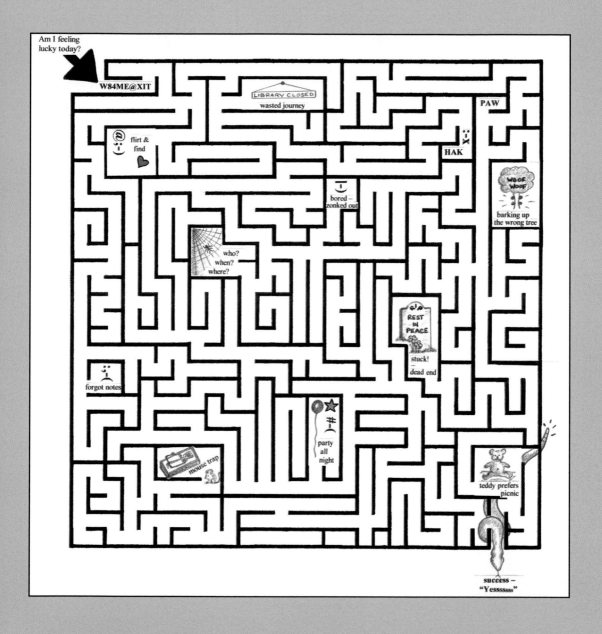

WHAT ARE RED, GREEN AND BLACK?

Civil registration in England and Wales first began on July 1st 1837, the same year that Princess Victoria became Queen. It is the recording of the birth, marriage and death of every man, woman and child. This requirement was ordered by the state or civil authority, hence its name. For many years a lot of births were not registered and it was not until 1875 that this became compulsory.

For easy recognition the certificates are normally coloured:

> **Red** …… for birth
> **Green** …. for marriage
> **Black** …. for death

It is important to know that although the procedures are very similar, Irish and Scottish civil registration is slightly different to that of England and Wales.

In Scotland, civil registration started on January 1st 1855. The certificate contains a little more information than that in England and Wales. The colour is usually beige.

Irish civil registration began on January 1st 1864. The certificates are white.

You will find that all these certificates — with the clues on them — will help you to delve into your past.

Until October 2007 we were able to view for ourselves the (paper) indexes in central London. These are large books containing the names in alphabetical order of everyone who was born, married or died . Sadly they are no longer available to the public. Do not be put off though as there are alternative ways of searching for those important certificates (see Chapter 4). These 2 photographs show the indexes before they were withdrawn and put into storage.

Left: The death indexes section.
Right: Vicky looking at the entry for her parents' marriage.

PARISH REGISTERS

During the reign of King Henry the Eighth, church administrators were ordered to keep records for their communities or parishes. They also kept registers for local events such as baptisms (christenings), marriages and burials. Very few of the earliest registers have survived. By 1598 the storage facilities had considerably improved, and the registers have more or less continued right up to the present day with the exception of 1649 to 1660. This was when Oliver Cromwell was ruling most of the country after the Civil War, and King Charles the First had been beheaded.

Top: A parish chest.

You may be interested to know that in 1667, to help the wool trade, a law was passed. It stated that all burials of the dead should be made in a woollen shroud or a fine of £5 had to be paid. In today's money that is about £550! For those that could not afford this, it was noted in the registers as 'naked', and a clergyman who turned a blind eye (ignored) for a fee was known as a 'naked priest'! Gradually this law was ignored and forgotten.

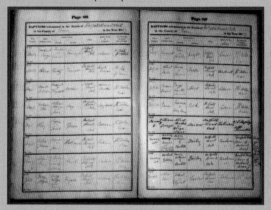

Pages from a baptism register of 1887.

Originally the parish registers were kept in locked parish chests in the church, but now most of them are stored at county record offices (CROs).

It will probably be a long time before you get to parish registers, so I do not intend to say any more about them here. You will learn as you go along and anyway most general books on family history will explain them further.

Points to remember

❖ Parish registers are early records of baptisms (christenings), marriages and burials.

❖ A parish is an area with its own church and priest.

❖ The parish chest was a strong, lockable chest (a container rather like a trunk) that contained the parish registers along with other important documents.

❖ A shroud is a piece of material that a dead body is wrapped in.

A 'fun' website that will work out the valuation of money from 1264 to 2007 is:
www.eh.net/hmit/ppowerbp/

CHAPTER 5

Taking the register

To put it as simply as possible, a census is the counting and listing of people. Imagine it as a sort of attendance register, similar to that taken every day in most British schools.

I have many times heard that the **whole** population of the **world** if standing close together would fit onto the Isle of Wight! If you find this island (off the south coast of England near Southampton and Portsmouth) on the map, you will find that statement very hard to believe. John (my husband), who likes maths and enjoys working out this sort of riddle, thinks that it is possible. We then took this a bit further and imagined that everyone in the world was invited to the Isle of Wight to be counted for a world census. Of course this is the most seriously stupid idea that you will have ever heard, but it does give your imagination a chance to run riot!

However, back to being sensible. Long ago there was a census when everyone had to go back to the place of his or her birth to be counted . . .

"And it came to pass in those days, that there went out a decree from Caesar Augustus, that all the world should be registered …. And all went to be registered, everyone into his own city". This is from the Bible, St Luke, Chapter 2.

Can you guess what this very well-known event was?

Joseph and Mary with the baby Jesus drawn by Flo.

"And Joseph also went up from Galilee, out of the city of Nazareth, into Judaea, unto the city of David, which is called Bethlehem to be registered with Mary his wife being great with child".

The rest of this story should be familiar to most of you. Joseph and Mary had to be registered (counted) too, so they went to Bethlehem, home of Joseph's ancestors, and Jesus was born in the city of David. Even if you do not celebrate Christmas, you will probably have heard about it.

The next important census (count) in history that could be of interest to you was completed in 1086.

As far as I know, most school children at some time during their school days learn about the famous Battle of Hastings in 1066, when King Harold's army was beaten. Legend tells us that he was killed with an arrow in his eye.

King Harold's grave at Waltham Abbey, Essex.

King Harold with an arrow in his eye at the Battle of Hastings, 1066.

This battle and the story leading up to it is shown on the very famous Bayeux Tapestry, which can still be seen today. This Bayeux Tapestry can be looked upon as the first-ever comic strip cartoon. William of Normandy (in northern France) became King William the First of England, or William the Conqueror. I know someone who can trace his ancestry back to this king.

William was his 30 x great-grandfather, but this is by no means unique. Many of us, if we (can) go back far enough will very probably come across someone who was well-known.

This new king ordered the written record of who owned what and its value — a survey of English landowners and their property - which was completed in 1086.

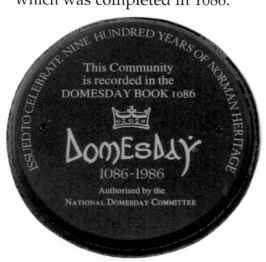

Above: King William the First ordering a survey of England.

Left: A plaque on the wall of a house.

Postcard reproduced with kind permission from Paul Johnson, Image Library Manager, The National Archives.

This first national census became known as Domesday Book, and is now kept at The National Archives (TNA) at Kew near London.

Since 1801 there has been a census taken every 10 years in the United Kingdom, with the exception of 1941, during the Second World War. A census is a count of every man, woman and child on a chosen day. After a census has been taken, the personal details are **not** available to the public for 100 years. Anyone born on or before Sunday 29th April 2001 (the most recent census day) will be on the 2001 Census — this includes everybody else that was alive that day. It is now locked away from most of us until January 2102. I don't think too many of us will be around then to see and refer to it, and no amount of Prince Charmings will wake up this Sleeping Beauty!

The Queen Mother, who died in March 2002, appears on the 1901 Census, and she will also appear on the 2001 Census because she lived until the age of 101. She was born on 4th August 1900, and died on 30th March 2002.

In August 1900, the same month that she was born, "Thirsty travellers were offered a syrupy drink" — this was Coca-Cola going on sale for the first time in Britain!

Vicky looking at the 1891 Census on a machine called a microfilm reader.

71

The 1841 Census, with the 1851, 1861, 1871, 1881, 1891 and the 1901 censuses for England and Wales, is kept at The National Archives in London. However, all the census returns from 1841 to 1901 have been microfilmed, and many local libraries and record offices have the censuses for their areas.

The Scottish census records for 1841 to 1901 are kept in New Register House, Edinburgh, and they are all available on the computer system.

The National Library of Wales at Aberystwyth has copies of the complete set of the Welsh census returns from 1841 to 1901.

Many of the census records in Ireland have not survived. However, both the 1901 (taken on 31st March) and 1911 (taken on 2nd April) censuses (which are almost complete) are available and kept in the National Archives of Ireland, in Dublin. The 1911 Census is available because of the destruction of so much earlier census material. Copies of the 1901 Census for the six northern counties in Ireland are available in the Public Record Office, in Belfast.

The dates — always on Sunday — for the censuses in England and Wales from 1841 are:

- 1841 — June 6th
- 1851 — March 30th
- 1861 — April 7th
- 1871 — April 2nd
- 1881 — April 3rd
- 1891 — April 5th
- 1901 — March 31st

The 1901 Census that was released — after 100 years — in January 2002, was supposed to start with a great fanfare because it was to have been published on the internet. Alas, this did not happen immediately because it proved to be too popular with several million people trying to access it at the same time. The whole computer system was unavailable for months, having crashed after the first few days leaving people still eagerly waiting for its release.

Now we can access the censuses from the comfort of our own homes by logging on to the following pay per view websites:

www.1901censusonline.com

www.ancestry.com

www.findmypast.com

My grandmother (Annie Florence Manley) mentioned in Chapter 4 appears on the 1901 Census. She is shown as living with both parents and all but one of her siblings. The youngest shown on the census —

Vicky looking at the 1901 Census on computer.

Name and surname of each person	Relation to head of family	Married or single	Age last birthday	Profession or occupation	Where born
Samuel W. Manley	Head	M	40	Surveyor of taxes	Cornwall, Gerrans
Martha A. Manley	wife	M	38		Kent, Sheerness
Bernard W. Manley	son	S	15		London, Greenwich
Vera R. Manley	dau	S	14		London, Brockley
Alice M. Manley	dau	S	12		London, Brockley
Harold G. Manley	son	S	11		London, Brockley
Gwynne Manley	son	S	9		Wales, Brecon
Annie F. Manley	dau	S	8		Wales, Brecon
Gwladus E. Manley	dau	S	6		Wales, Brecon
Walter J. Manley	son	S	3		Flint, Rhyl
Dorothy M. Manley	dau	S	7 months		Flint, Rhyl

Details from the Manley family from the 1901 Census. Annie (Florence), my grandmother is shown aged 8.

Dorothy Madge (known to everyone as Midge) was 7 months. Phyllis had not yet been born.

I helped to deliver the census forms for the 1991 Census in the area where I live. For this I was called an 'enumerator'. I quite enjoyed it and discovered all sorts of houses tucked away that I never knew existed.

I did find that a lot of people were quite reluctant to fill in the census forms because they felt that they were being spied on. However, these population surveys are necessary for planning for future schools, hospitals and other services. We know that many of our ancestors objected to filling them in, but we also know that some of the information that they contain is of great value to family historians.

Many people were not too keen on giving their correct age in 1991. This also applied to the past, because you had to have reached a certain age to join the army and to marry without parental permission. Adding a few years to your correct age was fairly common, so you must remember that it was dead easy to tell a thumping great porky! Be aware of this too when searching for a person's birth; as it could be well worth looking for a few 'extra' years either side of the supposed date of birth if they are not found immediately.

Enumerators collecting census details the day after the census, which was on April 7th 1861. Reproduced from The Leisure Hour, 1861.

If you watch the television programme *Blue Peter* (which I do!), you will occasionally hear the presenters asking for our help to count certain animals or birds. This is because a census is being taken on the population of that particular animal or bird. In April 2004 we learned from a census of birds that the numbers of both house sparrows and song thrushes has dropped alarmingly. This census has shown that the decline has been most rapid in the towns, with petrol, pesticides and the family cat taking most of the blame. This particular count was named Big Garden Bird Watch, and we were asked to spend one hour watching and recording all species of birds during the weekend of 25th/26th January. According to the bird census of 2006, the Goldfinch (a songbird) is now making a comeback to our gardens because of better quality food put out on the bird table. For the census of 2007 we have been informed that many of the smaller garden birds are disappearing because of that cackling black and white bird - the Magpie.

Perhaps this will become an annual survey now, especially with the current predictions of global warming.

During the year 2000 there was a census on 'What the Cat Brings in' organised by the Essex Naturalist Trust. This was to take a census on the estimated number of small animals in the county of Essex. We are told that counting 'Tiddles's feathered and four-footed furry trophies is apparently a very good way to get a realistic figure. At the time, we were asked by our vet friend either to record or store in the freezer any little corpses that we found, so that they could be checked and counted. How manky is that! The last time that this particular count was taken was in the year 1900.

Just in case you are wondering . . . no, we did not store anything in our freezer other than the usual frozen peas etc . . . !

'Swan Upping' is a sort of census. This ceremony held on behalf of the Queen takes place on London's River Thames every year. It consists of the catching and marking the baby swans to identify their owners, because many of them traditionally belong to The Crown (the King or Queen).

Farm animals are also marked in different ways, so that the farmers can identify their own animals. Their coats or ears are usually marked with a number or a coloured symbol so that they can roam freely and together over the countryside. *Winter Holiday* by Arthur Ransome (who wrote *Swallows and Amazons*) tells us of Dick rescuing the 'cragfast' sheep. He knew which farmer owned it because of the red mark on its shoulder.

Occasionally your family might be asked to take part in a traffic census; this is the counting of cars, lorries etc... Our town planners want to know how they can improve certain roads and routes, and it helps them to know exactly what particular type of traffic is already using them — and when.

Number 33 (Eleanor) and 24 (Harebell) can be recognised by the farmer who owns them.

Swan Upping.
Photographs: Robert Dean

Primary and secondary state schools have to complete a census every January, to find out exactly how many children are in full-time education.

It has been reported recently in some of the newspapers that the number of rats in Britain at the moment equals the human population. Therefore, there must have been some sort of ratty census, so think about it … for every one of us there is a rat lurking somewhere!

Important points to remember

- A census is the official count or list — mainly of people.
- 'Archives' is another word for collection of records or documents, and where they are kept.
- A century is a period of 100 years.
- Microfilm is a roll of film that has images from books and documents recorded on it.
- An enumerator is a person who delivers and collects the census forms.
- 'Census returns' is another way of describing the completed census forms.

MORE ANAGRAMS

1.	EVIL STARE	CERTIFICATES
2.	FOREST	UNCLE
3.	DUNGARIA	GENERATION
4.	CLUNE	GRAVEYARD
5.	TUNA	RELATIVES
6.	FIERCE IT CATS	LIBRARY
7.	O'TANGERINE	FAMILY TREE
8.	AFTER EMILY	FOSTER
9.	RILYBRA	AUNT
10.	GRAVY DEAR	GUARDIAN

FUN AND INTERESTING WEBSITES

Look at the famous Bayeux Tapestry at:
www.hastings1066.com

and the equally famous Domesday Book at:
www.domesdaybook.co.uk

THE NATIONAL ARCHIVES (TNA)

The National Archives at Kew.

There are record offices in most counties in England and Wales as well as many in Ireland and Scotland. They are usually called County Record Offices (**CROs** — not to be confused with **GROs**), although some are now changing their names to Archive Offices. Again, it is always advisable to prepare yourself well before a visit. Most of these record offices will have their own websites, but if you need to find them in *The Phone Book* they are usually listed under their local county council.

You will not be doing your family history for too long before you'll want to visit a CRO to continue with the filling in of your puzzle. These collections of mainly, local records (also called archives) vary considerably from area to area so it really is worth doing the advanced planning.

I am not going to say too much about The National Archives (TNA), which used to be called the Public Record Office (PRO). However I cannot miss it out, as it is such an important place for family historians. It used to be in the middle of London, which was fairly easy to get to. Now it is at Kew and, although still part of London, it's not nearly so central. Again, as mentioned in the last chapter, family history societies are frequently organising visits to TNA. These trips are not only fairly inexpensive, but all the hassle of getting there is already done for you, although the downside is that they are often in term time. That older friend or relative that I suggested in Chapter 4 could turn out to be a truly wonderful assistant!

I will not even begin to list some of the records that are kept at Kew, as there are so many. Check out their website for yourselves at www.nationalarchives.gov.uk If you click on 'Getting started' you should find a 'Just for kids' section.

There are over 100 miles of shelving containing thousands of so many amazing records (the distances between Birmingham and Liverpool, and York and Liverpool are both 102 miles). Lots of them will probably be of subjects that you have never heard of — yet.

For your visit you will need some sort of identification. The shop at TNA has quite a large range of family history books for sale along with other items. However, you must be aware that this will not be like a shop in your nearest shopping centre crammed with the latest knick-knacks!

When you order any documents to look at, everything is organised in such a way that you do not have to hang around and waste time for them to arrive. Other things can be looked at or checked, or you can go and get something to eat in the quite well stocked café.

If you do plan a trip to TNA at Kew, remember to check (on the website or by phoning) that it is open on the day of your proposed visit. Also check that there is no age restriction.

Remember: Do not confuse **CROs** (County Record Offices) with **GROs** (General Register Offices).

IN 1900 WHEN THE QUEEN MOTHER WAS BORN . . .

❖ Queen Victoria was still alive (she died in 1901)

❖ The tallest building in the world was the Eiffel Tower in Paris, France

❖ Great Britain was fighting a war (called the Boer War) in South Africa until 1902. The First World War did not start until the 4th August 1914 — her 14th birthday

❖ TV had not been invented - black and white was first broadcast in 1926, the year Princess Elizabeth (our present Queen) was born. Marmite (love it or loathe it!) had not been invented — until 1902

❖ The vacuum cleaner (Hoover to many of us) had not been invented

❖ The *Titanic* (the unsinkable liner that hit an iceberg) had not been built — it was launched in 1912 and sank on April 15th the same year

❖ There was no National Health Service (until 1948)

❖ 'Teddy bears' did not have this name until 1902 when President Theodore ("Teddy") Roosevelt of the United States refused to shoot a bear cub

❖ Walt Disney (who introduced *Mickey Mouse* and friends) was not born until December 1900

❖ Kellogg's Cornflakes and ice-cream cones had not been invented

❖ There were no biros because plastic had not been invented

❖ There were no 'talking pictures', that is cinema films with sound, until 1929. Up to then it was the 'silent movies'

❖ *Winnie the Pooh* with friends Piglet, Eyeore and Tigger had not been written about

❖ Women were not allowed to vote until 1918. In New Zealand — the first country to do so — women had been given the vote 25 years earlier

❖ Penicillin had not been discovered until 1928. It was not used as a medicine until 1940, and is now widely used to treat infection

❖ Man had not trekked to the North Pole until 1909; nor had the South Pole been reached until 1912

.... 100 years ago people were extremely polite and formal? You would find some of the rules for courting very quaint and funny, for example, when a young man took a young lady 'out', there would have been one of her family or friends tagging along to make sure that they all behaved properly with no touching at all ... so hanky-panky was a no go area!

This used to happen when my great-uncle met and, started 'stepping out' with my great-aunt Phyllis. Aunt Midge (the older sister of Phyllis) **had** to go everywhere with them and was looked upon as the 'escort'! Poor Aunt Midge thought Uncle Ray fancied her, but he loved Auntie Phyllis and married her. Sadly, Aunt Midge never married, and died in 1993 in a nursing home in Cornwall.

CHAPTER 6

Tinker, tailor, soldier, sailor . . .

"What do you want to be when you grow up?" seems to be one of the standard questions asked by the grown-ups over a 'certain age'.

If you stop to think … just about everything that anybody did (or does) will almost certainly have been in some way connected with an occupation. Even those at leisure will more than likely be having others serving them in one way or another, for example shop assistants, publicans, waitresses, life-guards and all the emergency services.

The same occupation was often passed down through the generations; it was (and still is, but not as often) quite common for father, son and even grandson to do the same sort of work.

The word 'occupation' can also be described as a profession, a trade, work, job or career. Most schools today have careers lessons included in the timetable and you may be familiar with The Careers Advisory Service.

During your search if you cannot find people where you were expecting to find them, knowing what they did for a living can be very helpful. For example, if you are looking for a William Jones and there are 3 William Jones, which one do you choose? Let us assume that your William Jones was a milkman, but you have no idea where he lived. Although the indexes do not reveal occupations (which are on the certificates), when you fill in a form to apply for the certificate you can add the known occupation, which will help the staff to select your correct William Jones — the milkman. This does sound rather complicated, but it is really quite simple especially after you have been shown what to do.

You will have already seen the column for occupation on the illustration of a certificate in Chapter 4 (page 53). If someone was a fisherman or a coast-guard for instance, that could be a clue that they might be living near the sea. Likewise, a coal miner would be found living in a mining area and a railway worker somewhere near the railway. Stories passed down through the family can help here as well; so it may be a good idea to just check up on that family gossip and rumour if you can.

Wills can be of great value to you, as occupations, as well as names, may be given. Not everyone made a will, although more have been made in recent years. However, if you discover that your ancestors did make any, they are likely to be very useful. As legal documents, they are probably far more accurate and reliable than some other records.

Wills after 1858 may be seen in the Probate Search Room, at the Principal Registry of the Family Division, High Holborn, in London.

Many occupations and trades have remained the same over the years like farmers, lawyers, doctors and the clergy, whilst others have all but disappeared. Examples of these include mining and steel manufacturing. A great many mines, pits and steel works across the country have closed down in the last 20 to 30 years. This is mainly because goods are produced more cheaply in other countries. Until 1946 there was no state aid or unemployment benefit that we have now. Areas that once buzzed with industrial activity suddenly had a massive amount of unemployment. A film called *The Full Monty* was based in Sheffield and illustrates this decline in employment.

A chemist shop.

Sheffield in the nineteenth century.

More recent times have seen the arrival of new occupations such as researchers and technologists. Today we have financial advisers, computer programmers, webmasters, sports psychologists and specialists in leisure and tourism. Who knows what different careers the future will bring?

There are many occupations from the past that you may not recognise at all. I did not know what a 'pattenmaker' was when I first saw it on my great-great-grandfather's marriage certificate. I discovered that he was a pattenmaker in 1859 — he made wooden shoes (pattens) with high heels, designed to keep the wearers' feet clean.

This factory in Rochdale (shown here in 1853) was owned by my husband's ancestors.

There will also be other trades that you may have never heard of because they are not in demand so much. Examples include thatchers and coopers (barrel makers).

Often people are prepared to travel all over the place to find work. Again this is no different from the past, although nowadays there is the Job Centre to help. In their search for work, our ancestors would move from one area to another to find and continue with their chosen trade. For example, tin miners from Cornwall were known to travel to the mining and industrial towns of the north of England and overseas in pursuit of work and a wage. It was often said that 'if there's a hole in the ground you'll find a Cornishman at the bottom of it'.

For example the 1861 census tells us that Abraham Price (age 36) and his wife Esther (age 34) had moved from a mining area of Cornwall to a lead mining area of the Lake District. They had had 8 children. In 1861 their two eldest sons, Abraham (14) and Isaac (12) were both recorded in this census as 'labourers at lead'.

This search for work is one of the main reasons for the movement of people over the centuries. This not only applied to travel within the United Kingdom but the rest of the world as well. Have you heard of the 'gold rush'? In the 19th century, gold had been discovered in places such as Australia, South Africa and California in America. People rushed to these areas to try their luck.

To take another example but for a very different reason, in Ireland there was a famine (shortage of food). For several years running the potato crop had failed because of a disease called potato blight, but 1845 was the worst year. Because potatoes were the principal diet, this crop failure caused misery, illness and death. As a result of this millions of people left Ireland to find work and hopefully a better and happier life. Who would have thought that the humble potato could have been responsible for such a dramatic change to peoples' lives?

A modern parallel is the continual drought, crop failures and consequent famine in the African countries of Sudan, Somalia and Ethiopia, some of the world's poorest places.

Have you heard of the Pilgrim Fathers? This group of people sailed to the 'New World' (North America) in the *Mayflower* in 1620 to escape religious persecution. They took with them their expertise in different trades and occupations, and started to make a new life for themselves. Had they not had the ability to work they could all have died very quickly.

Another very big group of constantly moving people are members of the armed services and their families. At The National Archives (TNA) at

The Pilgrim Fathers.

Kew — mentioned on page 78 — there are thousands and thousands of records relating to people in these services.

When I was at boarding school we used to count the number of plum or cherry stones that we had left on our pudding plates. We would say "Tinker, tailor, soldier, sailor, rich man, poor man, beggar man, thief". However many stones there were told us which of these men we would marry! Harmless fun, but it does make you think about some of those occupations mentioned.

A gypsy camp in 1901.

A tinker is another word for a gypsy. I much prefer the word gypsy though, and it's rumoured to have originally come from the word 'Egyptian'. They are also sometimes referred to as Romanies or travellers. One theory is that gypsies came from Egypt a long, long time ago before they travelled around the world selling their goods. However it is far more likely that they originated from northern India. They are frequently on the move but appear to be free and happy people who made music wherever they went. They became well known for making clothes pegs, fortune telling and selling heather for good luck — all of which they continue to do today. They were also associated with other occupations such as chair-bottomers, horse-dealers and braziers (that is working with a metal called brass, not making bras).

A member of our family travelled with gypsies in Europe after the First World War. He took his fiddle (violin) and first joined

A stove inside a gypsy caravan.

the Spanish gypsies; then went on to join the gypsies in Hungary and Romania.

Many gypsies do not celebrate marriage or Christmas (like some religions around the world); nor do they necessarily believe in a religion. A teacher friend of mine had to guess the ages of gypsy children in her class as they did not celebrate their birthdays either, and nobody had a clue as to how old they were.

Other nomadic (wandering) people would have included traders, pedlars, entertainers, market, and fair and circus folk.

A tailor is a person who makes, mends and alters clothes. Throughout history we have needed to wear clothes — mainly because of our climate, I guess. The thought of wearing a suit of armour in the Middle Ages over a 'birthday suit' (stark naked body) would have made most men cringe! During the same period there used to be travelling tailors, who, to keep warm, often slept under the material of the garments that they were making.

The rich and well off were particularly keen on wearing the latest fashions made from the finest materials. This is incredibly similar to many people of today with all their latest designer clothes.

A tailor and his apprentices.

The Victorians did not like ankles or legs to show, so girls' and womens' dresses and skirts were all long. Trousers were mainly worn by the men at this time. Very few girls wore them, with few exceptions such as Lancashire pit-girls. Incidentally, the bra was not invented until 1889 in Paris, and it was a long time before they were marketed in the UK. My mum can remember winding elastic around herself to try and stop the bouncy bits from bouncing too much! The Victorians who took this 'leg-hiding' to ridiculous extremes (or so it seems to us now) even used to drape material around the legs of furniture. You can see this in the photograph of a Victorian sitting room as well as the Victorian love of decoration; with every available space crammed full of knick-knacks.

Early twentieth century fashions.

A Victorian sitting room.

To return to the armed forces. A soldier is someone who serves in an army. An army is a collection of men and, nowadays women, who train together to defend land, property and people. They may fight in wars and battles in different parts of the world. You may have heard of the Gulf War of 1991 and of the more recent war in Iraq in 2003. We are now often hearing about the Royal Marines. Although they are part of the army today, they were previously the fighting force of the Royal Navy.

Do any of your family remember the Second World War?

"What did you do in the war?" is a frequently asked question. We all want to know what our parents, grandparents and other relatives actually did; perhaps out of interest and curiosity, as well as wanting to know for the purpose of our family histories. Please remember though my warning in Chapter 1 that not everybody will want to talk about their (wartime) experiences.

Your older relatives may even recall stories that have been passed down from the Great War otherwise known as the First World War. The stories of carol singing, and a game of football played on Christmas Day 1914 between British and German soldiers are true. My grandfather was there, and yes, the following day they all went back to shooting at each other.

A sailor is someone who serves in a ship at sea. The Royal Navy is the name of the navy of the United Kingdom that, like the army, defends its country at sea. Sailors also earn their living by working on cargo and passenger ships. These ships are part of the Merchant Navy.

Hundreds of years ago when men were needed to fight in the navy and did not want to go, they were 'press-ganged', which means that they were kidnapped. Can you imagine having just a tad too much of a good time with your mates on Friday night? You then might wake up on Saturday morning surrounded by sea heading for somewhere that you had never heard of! That actually happened; but thank goodness it does not happen today.

Very recently I had a conversation with an elderly lady, who told me that her great-great-grandfather was kidnapped in France. It appears that as a child (yes, a five-year old child, but this **was** a long time ago) he was taken from his parents, put onto a warship and used as a 'powder monkey'. Small people were needed for this dangerous work because they could move about the ship quickly. This involved carrying the gunpowder to the men firing the cannons at the enemy.

We celebrated the anniversary of the Battle of Trafalgar on Trafalgar Day (21st October) in 2005. The Admiral, Lord Nelson, would have had powder monkeys on board his ship the *Victory* as well as the other ships of the English fleet in 1805.

Above: The boy on the right, although not really tiny, could have been a powder monkey.

Left: A crossing sweeper.

A recently published book written by Paul Dowswell called *Powder Monkey* tells us of a lad called Sam who was press-ganged and became a powder monkey. Although this is not a true story it does tell us what life on a Royal Navy man-of-war was like.

Another new book written by Tony Robinson called *The Worst Children's Jobs in History* mentions powder monkeys. He includes a lot of other **really** nasty jobs that children were made to do such as 'gong-scourers'. This was clearing out filthy, smelly pits of human sewage making that paper round of today look wonderful in comparison. His book also tells you about the grown-up called Baldwin Le Pettour who became the Royal Farter!

Another horrible job was a 'crossing sweeper' who cleared a path through dirty streets which included horse poo; this enabled people to cross the roads without getting their feet mucky.

Yet another was a 'mudlark' who spent time around river-banks containing stinking sewage, rats and dead animals looking for anything that could be sold to make money.

I must mention the Royal Air Force here. Although a fairly new branch of the United

The Mudlark.

Kingdom's fighting forces, it played an unforgettable part in the Second World War. Since 1918 it has been as important a part of our nation's defence as the Army, the Royal Navy and all other fighting units.

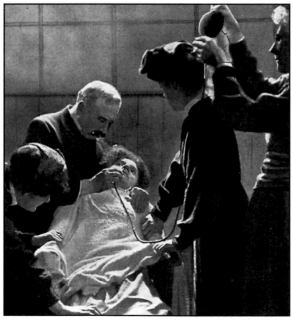

A suffragette in prison being force fed because she was on hunger strike.

Before the First World War few middle-class women worked. Generally most women were given little chance to discuss anything of importance and were not even allowed to vote until 1918. Can you imagine that happening now? "No way!" I hear all the girls saying.

The vote for women came about because men were so impressed by all the work done by them during this war; and perhaps they didn't want the suffragettes smashing the place up again . . . which some of them did in their determination to be allowed to vote.

Whilst many of the men were away fighting, the women back at home were doing much of the work normally done by the men.

Nowadays more women work than in the past. This can be seen by the number of mums who return to work as soon as possible after the birth of their babies; or when the children reach school age.

Points to remember

❖ A famine is a drastic shortage of food.
❖ Records for the armed services (including the Air Force, Army and Navy) are kept at The National Archives at Kew.
❖ There will be records kept somewhere on just about everything that has been mentioned in this chapter and the next one. I do not intend to give any further information (except a few addresses at the end), because there is just not the room. Please do not give up though — do some further reading or just find someone and ask.
❖ Suffragettes were women who aggressively campaigned for the right to vote.

MUDDLED MEANINGS

Can you match these occupations with their correct description?

1.	haberdasher	a. makes & mends barrels
2.	costermonger	b. maker & seller of women's hats
3.	apothecary	c. someone who sells fruit & vegetables from a barrow
4.	corsetière	d. sells ribbons, sewing & dressmaking materials
5.	ironmonger	e. someone who makes pots & dishes
6.	confectioner	f. someone who makes & sells medicines
7.	milliner	g. a shoe maker and mender
8.	cooper	h. a maker, fitter & seller of corsets
9.	potter	i. someone who sells metal tools & utensils
10.	cobbler	j. someone who makes & sells sweets

My grandfather Cecil Richard Pearse was wounded during the First World War but he was one of the lucky ones because he came home to live for many years.

The message on the card reads:
"Cecil is wounded and is at present at No. 4. General Hospital B.1. Surgical Ward. British Expeditionary Force.

He doesn't say much beyond he is wounded with pieces of shell in his thighs and had to be transferred by stretcher, train, motor etc. to his present address."

Cecil Richard Pearse (marked with a cross) who served with Queen Victoria's Rifles at the beginning of the First World War.

Top:
British cemetery at Passchendaele.

Above left:
How a First World War trench looks in 2004.

Above right:
German cemetery at Langemark.

Left:
"Our Jimmy" born in France and served the 1st Scottish Rifles as a mascot, buried in Central Park, Peterborough, Cambridgeshire.
Photograph: Peter Watson

Right:
Careless talk can cost lives.

CHAPTER 7

Rich man, poor man, beggar man, thief

To continue with the 'cherry stones': —
The rich man should mean to you girls exactly what it says! How many of us dream of marrying someone with stacks of money and, then what happy bunnies we would be. Would we have been happy though? In the past many girls or young ladies lived in misery, having pleased their parents by getting married only for the money and the lifestyle that went with it. Occasionally some of them might have been prepared to marry any old wealthy duffer just to get away from the drudgery of home life. They probably thought that things could not get worse, but they often did.

Most upper-class men simply did not work. They may have inherited their wealth or built up a prosperous business very probably using child or slave labour. They would often own a great house with lots of servants and spend a great deal of time in the countryside enjoying outdoor sports such as hunting, hawking, shooting and fishing. The rich man would have his own carriage, and spend time travelling around the country with his family visiting other rich and fashionable friends. It would have been extremely important to him to be seen at times of great social activity (to us this would mean lots of parties), so he'd travel to the towns and cities for these events such as the London Season.

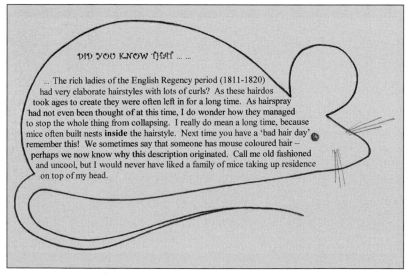

DID YOU KNOW THAT ... ...

... The rich ladies of the English Regency period (1811-1820) had very elaborate hairstyles with lots of curls? As these hairdos took ages to create they were often left in for a long time. As hairspray had not even been thought of at this time, I do wonder how they managed to stop the whole thing from collapsing. I really do mean a long time, because mice often built nests **inside** the hairstyle. Next time you have a 'bad hair day' remember this! We sometimes say that someone has mouse coloured hair – perhaps we now know why this description originated. Call me old fashioned and uncool, but I would never have liked a family of mice taking up residence on top of my head.

This can be seen now with the annual stampede to events like the Chelsea Flower Show and Royal Ascot. The yearly journey to the Glastonbury and Isle of Wight Festivals for the often, muddy knees-up, is an example of the modern person who wants to be seen at all the right places.

Many of the rich ladies would have seen very little of their children. Even from birth some babies were handed over to the 'wet nurse' who was the person employed to breastfeed for her! They would then have been passed on to a nanny, followed by the governess, rather like pass the parcel. Before the children were 10, they would have been looked after by at least three different people, who probably knew them

Wealthy people visiting the poor.

better than their own parents.

To earn a living, the unmarried women who needed employment, but were not really poor, often found work as nannies, nursery nurses or governesses. The actual work would be very similar to the modern nanny and they probably would have lived in the same house as the family. Their room would have been at the top of the house near the nursery. They would have had

Children helping in the kitchen.

The poor, queuing.

their meals, either with the children or with the other servants in the basement — 'below stairs'. More than likely, they would have sent most of their wages back home.

The middle-class women-folk were much undervalued, and were expected to do all the domestic duties as well as produce and bring up the babies. Families tended to be large because there was no efficient contraception. My grandmother (Annie Florence Manley) was one of 10 children. She could clearly remember hearing her mother crying with despair on discovering that she was pregnant once again.

The poor man and the beggar man are probably not quite the husbands or partners that you had in mind. Poor people wouldn't have had many belongings, money, or extra clothes. To put it bluntly, beggars probably had nothing except the

A young servant girl.

rags they were wearing. They probably did not even know their real names, if they had them.

The lives of the poor would be spent looking after and serving others, with very little time for themselves.

In the houses of the rich they could be found working downstairs in the kitchens as servants. The 'necessary woman' was a servant responsible for the

Agricultural labourers known as 'ag labs'.

emptying and cleaning of chamber pots. In the country they could be working as farm labourers. During your research you will very probably see and hear the words 'ag lab' many times. No this was not text messaging, it is short for 'agricultural labourer'.

The kitchen in Ramsey Museum, photographed by Sue Fearn. A similar bath to the one seen hanging on the wall can be seen later in Chapter 10.

I briefly mentioned domestic service in my Introduction. Betty, a friend of mine who is 79, often talks about her years spent 'in service'. Your parents and grandparents might remember a TV programme of the 1970s called *Upstairs Downstairs*. This gave the viewer a good idea of early 20th century life in a fairly wealthy family 'upstairs'; and their servants who lived 'downstairs'. All these servants from the head male servant called a butler, the cook, chauffeur (driver) and senior parlour maid down to the 'tweeny' (the maid who worked for the servants) would have worked extremely hard. They got up very early and would have fallen into a shared bed in the attic, tired and exhausted at the end of a very long day. A few hours rest with little warmth, and very few interests or games to play became the daily routine . . . and so their lives went on with little to look forward to. Many employers even forbade their servants to have boy or girlfriends. It must have been extremely difficult to 'go out' with someone, without the household suspecting 'hanky-panky'.

Today we are extremely lucky compared with the millions of unfortunate people over the years. The majority of them would probably have had one day off a year, and that was Christmas Day (except for the domestic servants). Children with poor backgrounds were pushed into work very early

Young boys going to work down the mine shaft.

FUN AND INTERESTING WEBSITES
A website about coal mining including pictures of pit-ponies:
www.cmhrc.co.uk

For crime and punishment look at the Old Bailey website
www.oldbaileyonline.org/schools

in their lives to help the family financially. This could have been some sort of apprenticeship when the master of a trade (for example a baker) would be paid for teaching the apprentice his trade in return for food, clothes and a roof over his head. This was a very cheap form of labour; children sometimes as young as seven had little protection from ill treatment and overwork as they frequently lived away from home.

The older apprentice was not even allowed to marry without his master's permission.

Both the mining industry and the factories employed a huge proportion of men and boys if they happened to live in mining or industrial areas. Young girls were employed as well in the factories. In places like the Midlands, Birmingham and Liverpool there were many of these

At the coal face.

factories. The owners of cotton mills in cities such as Manchester, Bradford and Leeds in the North of England were particularly notorious for their harsh treatment.

The rat-catcher working in a sewer.

Child performers had better lives. They were sometimes known as 'Footlight Fairies' and appeared on stage in pantomime, the theatre and the music halls. This was big business in the 1880s and children as young as six and seven were employed. Although they were often exhausted, on the whole there appeared to be very little physical abuse. A child, when earning, was considered a very important member of the household and was therefore generally treated well at home. On 'pay day' parents usually

99

A Manchester factory.

managed to collect them from work; it would be nice to think that this was concern for their safety, but I suspect the concern was for the money!

Another name for a poor man is a 'pauper'. Many paupers lived in workhouses, some of which started in the 17th century, where they were given food and lodgings. An Act of Parliament in 1834 led to the more severe Union Workhouses, where the able inmates were expected to work hard for their keep. Many of them were dreadfully harsh places with a prison like appearance and very strict rules. Until 1929 they took in the poor of all ages, from

A wealthy family going to see the 'footlight fairies' at the pantomime.

From "THE VILLAGE" by George Crabbe

Theirs is yon house that holds the parish-poor,
Whose walls of mud scarce bear the broken door;
There, where the putrid vapours, flagging, play,
And the dull wheel hums doleful through the day;—
There children dwell who know no parents' care;
Parents, who know no children's love, dwell there!
Heartbroken matrons on their joyless bed,
Forsaken wives, and mothers never wed;
Dejected widows with unheeded tears,
And crippled age with more than childhood fears;
The lame, the blind, and, far the happiest they!
The moping idiot and the madman gay.

Written in 1783

FUN AND INTERESTING WEBSITE
An ancestor may have experienced the workhouse:
www. workouses.co.uk

Top: Typical appearance of the waifs and strays that ended up in the workhouse. Above: Coleshill Workhouse, Warwickshire. Drawings: Val Preece

babies to the elderly. Both Ireland and Scotland also had similar Poor Laws.

Workhouses must not be confused with 'almshouses'. Most almshouses were founded during the Middle Ages, and supported by charity; they provided accommodation for the poor and the elderly. In many towns and villages today there are old buildings that are referred to as 'the old almshouses'. Some of them are still lived in.

Captain Thomas Coram, founder of the Foundling Hospital.

A Victorian courtroom.

The abandoning of babies had become very common in the 18th century. They were called foundlings. It was usual to leave them in a place where they would be found very quickly.

A friend of mine has an ancestor who was left on the doorstep of the Foundling Hospital in 1759. When she made enquiries she found that the records of this hospital still exist. She also found with these records a piece of clothing that the child was wearing on arrival — that is nearly 250 years ago!

We still have children's homes today. Of the many, you may recognise the name of Dr Barnardo's who still have all their records.

Above: Stocks at Warwick Castle.

Left: A Victorian policeman's truncheon and an Irish constabulary whistle.

Top: A hanging scene from the Calender of Prisoners, 1778-1844. Reproduced courtesy of Oxfordshire Record Office.

Above: a ducking stool.

Right: The Caxton Gibbet near Cambridge. This was an extreme form of punishment, the offender, and very often innocent victim, would have died.

The beggar man had nowhere to live. They would have sheltered anywhere outside that they could find to get away from the weather — be it hot or cold. They got the name of beggar, because they would beg (ask or plead) for food and money (alms) from people who were better off than them.

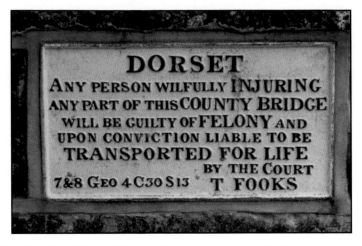

A thief is one who steals. In the film *Oliver*, Fagin teaches the homeless children to pick pockets. In real life if caught, they would have been thrown into prison. Have you heard the saying 'in clink'? Among the many prisons in London there was one called the Clink.

Many convicts were transported (sent) to other parts of the world as a form of punishment. Transportation began as early as 1620 when prisoners were sent to America. Later on they were sent to Australia after America fought to gain its independence in 1776. Some would have committed a serious offence and deserved punishment. However for others, their only crime was stealing a pig, a handkerchief or even a loaf of bread for the starving wife and children. Transportation finally stopped in 1868. There are today in Australia and New Zealand thousands of people whose ancestry can be traced back to some poor soul who had been sent there in a convict ship. Many people died during these long voyages, which lasted for months. The conditions on board were dreadful so next time you feel like a herded animal on a cross-channel ferry just count your blessings!

This is not quite theft, but I know someone with an ancestor called 'Uncle Albert' from Yorkshire. In 1894 his death certificate had the cause of death written down as … "Dislocation of the neck by hanging under sentence of law". He was hanged for the killing of an infant, a crime to which his wife later confessed on her deathbed.

Many parts of the country are (or were) well known for their local industries. I have already talked about miners from Cornwall and the great industrial towns from the north with their factories and mills. Places near the sea tended to concentrate on the fishing industry, while the ports dealt with trading (exporting and importing of goods) with other countries. The ports with all the dockyard jobs have now declined, or even closed down because of aircraft being used more and more for the carrying of freight (goods or cargo). These coastal areas are now popular with the leisure and tourism industry. The Potteries, a region near Stoke-on-Trent became the centre for English pottery making. A friend lives in Occupation Lane in Nottingham; this town is famous for its lace making. Kent (sometimes called the garden of England), produces most of the hops that are used in beer making; both Cheddar and Stilton, are famous for their cheeses and Northampton is a shoe-making area — hence Northampton Town Football Club having the nick-name of 'Cobblers' . . . because a cobbler is a shoe maker.

You might have noticed that, despite everything written in Chapters 6 and 7, I have left hundreds of occupations out. There are far too many to list here, however, records do exist for many of them. There are records for the clergy, medical workers, lawyers, the police, firemen, teachers and even politicians, to coastguards, railwaymen, gamekeepers and lock keepers, to name but a few. Lock keepers worked the locks on canals.

A girls' school room.

Boys in a school room.

Rugby School. Photograph: John Chard, a member of the Rugby Family History Group.

Schoolroom in Ramsey Museum. Photographed by Sue Fearn.

I feel that I cannot leave this chapter without briefly mentioning education — don't worry, it will be brief!

A good many of the famous schools that we hear about today were originally started for poor boys (did you notice — **only** boys, and Rugby School being one of them. What game was invented there in 1823, I wonder?). Before education was provided by the state, the church was involved with setting up schools. Compared with the number there are now, there were very few, as a large proportion of children never attended school.

By 1876 the government required all children to have a basic education. However, it was not until 1880 that attending a school up to the age of 10 became compulsory. The school truancy inspector was called a 'kidcatcher'.

Important points to remember

- ❖ To inherit is to receive money, goods or property from someone who has died. A legal document called a will is written before a person's death. This states how they want their possessions to be distributed after their death.
- ❖ A wet nurse was a woman employed to breastfeed another's child. She would have either recently had a baby or her baby had died.
- ❖ Contraception is the prevention of pregnancy.
- ❖ An apprentice is someone working for another in exchange for being taught a trade.
- ❖ Physical abuse (as well as mental abuse) is another way of saying bullying.
- ❖ Workhouses were institutions that gave the poor of all ages somewhere to live. Those that were able, had to work to earn their keep, but the very young, the elderly and the sick were also allowed to live in them.
- ❖ An almshouse was a house provided by charity (normally the church) for the poor and elderly.
- ❖ A foundling was a baby deserted at birth. The parents were usually not known.
- ❖ Transportation was the sending of prisoners to a British Colony overseas in a prison ship.

DO ANY MEMBERS OF YOUR FAMILY REMEMBER THE SECOND WORLD WAR 1939-1945?

Ask your grandparents and other older relatives if they can remember:

- ❖ Sweet rations
- ❖ Making your own ice cream with custard!
- ❖ Food rationing & having no oranges or bananas
- ❖ Collecting nuts, berries, wild mushrooms, stinging nettles (yes, to eat!) and dandelion leaves from the countryside
- ❖ Clothes rationing
- ❖ The bath water was to be no deeper than 5 inches (12 cms)
- ❖ Petrol rationing, and no signposts on the roads. People walked or used bicycles whenever possible
- ❖ The Blackout — so lights on the ground could not be seen from the air
- ❖ Having gas masks with them at all times
- ❖ Advertisements with the slogan 'Dig for Victory' — this meant to produce as much home grown food as possible
- ❖ The Land Army — where girls and women worked on the land to produce food
- ❖ Collecting conkers in autumn. They were used in the making of explosives during both World Wars

Black cows being painted so that they will be seen more easily by motorists at night.

© PA Photos

- ❖ Sitting round a crackly radio listening to news of the war
- ❖ The American soldiers bringing luxuries such as nylon stockings with them, when they came over to Britain after joining the war
- ❖ Girls drawing lines down the back of their legs with black crayon to look as if they were wearing stockings
- ❖ Evacuees — at the beginning of the war, children in the big towns were sent away from their families to the countryside to escape the bombing. Many were also sent abroad to 'safe' places such as Canada
- ❖ The Home Guard — do older members of your family enjoy *Dad's Army*?
- ❖ Air raid sirens, air raids and air raid shelters
- ❖ When newspapers had been read, they were cut up into squares and used for loo paper
- ❖ Underwear being made out of faulty parachutes

A week's ration for one adult (except for the jam).

WARTIME FOOD RATIONS FOR ONE ADULT

Butter: 2 oz (50 g) a week
Meat: to the value of 6 pence in today's money
Cheese: 2oz (50 g) a week
Bacon & ham: 4 oz (100 g) a week
Magarine: 4 oz (100 g) a week
Sugar: 8 oz (225 g) a week
Cooking fat: 4 oz (100 g) a week
Tea: 2 oz (50 g) a week
Milk: 2 — 3 pints a week
Jam: 1lb (1 jar) every 2 months
Eggs: 1 egg a week
Sweets: 12oz (350 g) every 4 weeks

The ration books are reproduced by kind permission of the Trustees of Priest's House Museum, Wimborne, Dorset.

FUN AND INTERESTING WEBSITES
Learn more about the World Wars from the Imperial War Museum at:
www.iwm.org.uk

A site that deals with British Armed Forces is
www.britisharmedforces.org

LIFE IN A SHELTER

Memories of an air raid by a 10 year old boy.

I'm in bed - Suddenly the air raid siren sounds. Dad comes up stairs and gets me out of bed. Suddenly I hear the German bombers coming over London we rush out into the back yard and in to our Anderson Shelter. mum opened the door we all went in. We sat down in the dark. Sounds of bombs dropping in the distance, the smells in the shelter were awful. I think a bomb hit our house because it was so near. We could hear the A.A. Guns firing in the back ground. I felt frightened suddenly a bomb bounced off our shelter my heart was beating. In the morning our house had not been bombed

A lady with her seven children settling down in the air raid shelter in the garden.

Photograph no. ZZZ9182c reproduced courtesy of the Imperial War Museum, London.

A child's Mickey Mouse gas mask. Photograph taken by the author with permission from Rhodes Memorial Museum, Bishop's Stortford.

STAR CROSSWORD

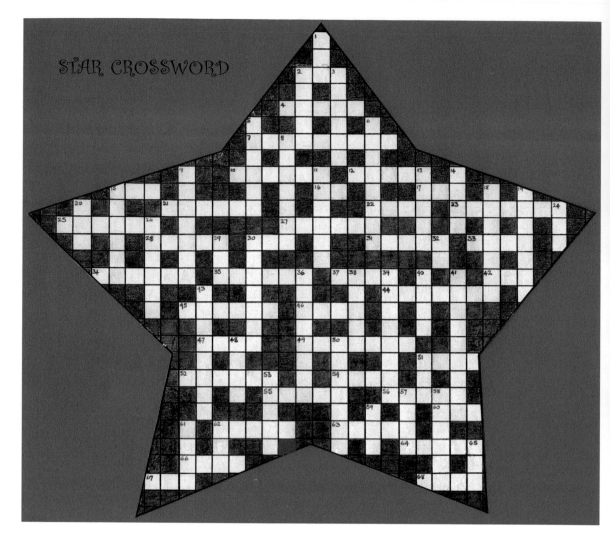

Across

2. Popular spinning toy (3)
4. Get-together with food, music and dance (5)
7. People you're descended from (9)
10. Teddies had one in the woods (6)
12. Opposite of queens (5)
15. A pig's home (3)
16. Short for hello (2)
17. Vehicle with 4 wheels (3)
21. —— crawlies (6)
22. Currency of most European Union countries (4)
23. Places for selling goods with stalls (7)
25. The movies (6)
27. Your chosen occupation (6)
28. —— and horses (5)
30. Worn on the head (3)
31. '——over' at your pal's house (5)
33. Opposite of shallow (4)
34. Someone accompanying another person (6)
35. Tittle-tattle (6)
37. Entrance with a curved roof (4)
42. Wild animals' home (3)
44. Children with no known parents (7)
45. Short for photographs (6)
46. You go to school during ——time (4)
47. My little —— (4)
49. Stored documents and archives (7)
51. Mind Your Own Business [txt] (4)
52. A male witch (6)
54. Cinderella had 2 —— sisters (4)
55. Uncles and —— (5)
56. Latest —— in fashion (5)
60. 'Organisation' in website & e-mail addresses (3)
62. Happiness or a teenage magazine (5)
63. Written record of every day in a small book (5)
64. Largest and very poor country in Africa (5)
66. Newest and youngest member of family (4)
67. Used to unlock (3)
68. Popular family card game (4)

Down

1. Park where animals are kept (3)
2. Draw an exact copy through thin paper (5)
3. —— blight was the cause of famine in Ireland (6)
5. —— tree (6)
6. Popular footwear of today (8)
8. Join together, or trying to '——— you' (7)
9. One who serves or works for others (7)
11. Sweet, angelic child with wings (6)
13. —— a goal (5)
14. Coat of —— in heraldry (4)
15. Rationing for these was ended in 1953 (6)
18. Mates (7)
19. Used in attacks, wars and battles for fighting with (7)
20. False hair (3)
24. Travel across snow (3)
26. Those who perform on stage and screen (6)
29. A female old bag! (3)
30. Study of the past (7)
32. Wee (small) word for a chamber pot (2)
36. Boy who never grew up (5,3)
38. Second son of Posh and Becks (5)
39. Pleasure trips away from home (8)
40. Computer junk mail (4)
41. The Pilgrim Fathers sailed in this ship in 1620 (9)
43. Modern girls love doing this 'till they drop! (8)
48. ——'s Ark (4)
50. Religious war (7)
51. Month of the year (3)
53. Author's loopy lurcher (5)
57. Children's playthings (4)
58. Capital of England (6)
59. —- masks were worn during the war (3)
61. Precious stone, also a girls' name (4)
62. Keeps your front clean when eating (3)
65. Short sleep or forty winks (3)

CHAPTER 8

What's in a name?

The first question to the proud parents on the birth of a new baby is "Is it a boy or is it a girl?" followed quickly by "What is he or she called?" The next questions are "When?" and "What is the weight?" but it is the name that most people are really interested in.

In 1952 the most popular names for children born in that year were David and Susan. The top two names in England in 2006 were Jack and Olivia, and in Wales Joshua and Megan. In Scotland in 2005, parents' favourite names were Lewis and Sophie, while Ireland's top two for that year were Jack and Katie. The name Mohammed is now beginning to be a popular name in England and Wales. Your name identifies you and makes you an individual, although you may still have to share it with others throughout the world. However, having a name makes everything less complicated — otherwise imagine the chaos if everybody in your class was called Fred or Freda Bloggs. No one would know whether they were being spoken to, nor could they single out someone else except with a pointed finger and a "Hey, you!"

A registrar told me recently that someone came in to register the birth of his new baby daughter. When asked for the name he began "Caroline, Amber, Mary, Beatrice … " until the first letter of each name spelt Cambridge — as in United, the football team!

In the search for your ancestors, it will not take you too long to realise that the more forenames (also called birth names and Christian names) a person has, the easier it should be to find them. This also applies if the names are slightly unusual. The birth certificates of Digby Sidebottom or Lettice Gotobed should be fairly simple to find. However, finding Emma Smith's birth may not be quite so easy as there could be many of them. Knowing the exact date of birth or the address would be helpful or, failing that, as talked about in Chapter 6, knowing the occupation of Emma Smith's parents could give you that vital clue. This will help you to find the correct Emma Smith and so go back another generation.

Very few people had 25 names like Ann Pepper who was born on 19th December 1882. Her parents Sarah Jane and Arthur Pepper (a laundryman) chose to call her: Ann, Bertha, Cecilia, Diana, Emily, Fanny, Gertrude, Hypatia, Inez, Jane, Kate, Louisa, Maud, Nora, Ophelia, Quince, Rebecca, Starkey, Teresa, Ulysis, Venus, Winifred, Xenophon, Yetty and Zeus. I hope she knew her alphabet after all that, but have you spotted the missing letter?

Names have evolved (developed) over time since the 12th and 13th centuries; and then nicknames were probably used more than surnames. Up until then it must have been a tad frustrating. Without a name how would your best mate have caught your attention that there was something large, hairy, hungry and very unfriendly lurking behind you?

Have you ever thought about your name? Have you wondered why you were given the name you have; were you named after a particular person and do you know what your names mean?

Names come into and go out of fashion. There is no pattern as to when a particular name will become popular again. At the moment it is fashionable to give children unusual names. Some babies are named after someone famous or after a favourite friend or relative. Apparently in Spring 2003 when Shane Richie joined the cast of *EastEnders* as the character Alfie Moon, Alfie immediately became a popular boys' name.

Over the years, many children have been named after members of royal families.

UNUSUAL NAMES

I am sure that you will have heard of some of these names:

Kylie Minogue & **Delta** Goodrem who both started out acting in *Neighbours*, the well-known Australian soap

Brooklyn, Romeo and **Cruz** Beckham

Apple the daughter of Gwyneth Paltrow

Blossom, the daughter of Kasey Ainsworth who played Little Mo in *EastEnders*

Cy and older brother **Flynn**, the sons of super-model Elle Macpherson

Peaches, and sisters **Fifi Trixibelle, Little Pixie** and **Heavenly Hiraani Tigerlily** are all daughters of Bob Geldof the singer and organiser of Live Aid.

Madonna with her children **Lourdes** and **Rocco**. She has now added to her family by adopting **David** from Malawi

Tallulah the daughter of Jessie Wallace, otherwise known as Kat Moon. She played Alfie's wife in *EastEnders*

Mackenzie the baby daughter of J K Rowling

Bluebell Madonna the daughter of Geri Halliwel, otherwise known as Ginger Spice

Shiloh Nouvel the daughter of Brad Pitt and Angelina Jolie; and sister of **Maddox, Zahara** and **Pax Thien**

Not only do well-known people sometimes choose unusual names for their children. This birth announcement was spotted in May 2004 — **Ruby Rhapsody Panda**, a new sister for **Mimi Magenta Poodle!**

Try doing a survey of the first names of all your friends. Collect as many names as possible, and then ask these friends to find out all their parents' names. You will probably find that these two lists are completely different, simply because of the naming pattern fashion at the time. You could even try making a list of their grandparents' names and again you should see a difference.

Surnames are also known as second names and family names. When women get married they usually replace their maiden surname with the surname of their new husband. This change of name takes place during the marriage service. Normally the bride will sign her 'old' name for the last time when she signs the register during the ceremony.

There are some exceptions, as many married women today choose to use their maiden surname.

A maiden name is a woman's family name before she marries, but to avoid confusion it is often referred to as 'maiden surname'.

These days more and more people get married more than once. Don't panic here with all the name changes, just take your time and try and work it out logically.

A lot of film and pop stars choose to use their maiden names. Also in many other cases, both men and women have a totally different name (a pen-name or stage-name) to the one they were given at birth. Do you recognise the name Reginald Kenneth Dwight? Maybe not, but do you know the name Elton John? Both these names are in fact those of Elton John — one he was born with, and the one we know him by. Would he have been as famous if he had kept the name Reginald?

Cilla Black is another example, as her 'real' name is Priscilla White. Cliff Richard who could still be the heart-throb of your grandmother was born Harry Webb; and the famous ballerina Darcey Bussell was once called Marnie Mercedes. Marilyn Monroe, whom I mention in Chapter 2, changed her name from Norma Jean Mortensen — somehow it does not sound quite so glamorous, does it?

Have you wondered where your surname originated? Many surnames or family names long, long ago evolved from the surroundings at the time. For example you might have been called 'Wood' if you happened to live — yes, you've guessed it — near a wood. There are many other names like this such as Field, Hill, Lake and Castle. Surnames also evolved from the type of work people did, for example Potter, Thatcher, Cooper and Carpenter. You may recognise two of these from Chapter 6 when I am talking about occupations and trades.

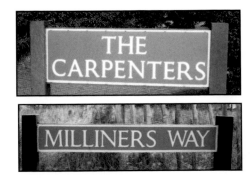

Street names depicting some occupations.

The longest name in the UK of a town. It is in Wales and means "St Mary's Church in the hollow of the white hazel near to the rapid whirlpool of Llantysilio of the red cave".

New names were frequently brought into the country by settlers (immigrants). This moving around from one place to another is called migration.

I have recently learnt (from TV's *Blue Peter*) that in India the surname 'Patel' used to mean a farmer.

Can you think of anyone you know who has the same surname as a town?

The chances are that their ancestors originally came from that area, and examples include York, Lincoln, Lancaster, Chester, Douglas and Dublin. We know a couple whose surname is O'Smotherly. Pat, the husband comes from Yorkshire where there just happens to be a town called Osmotherley. Similarly, although

Emigrants from Europe arriving in New York, USA.

114

fictional, could Albert Sandwich have been named after Sandwich in Kent? He was Carrie's friend in the book *Carrie's War* by Nina Bawden. When our ancestors emigrated to begin new lives overseas, they took many place names with them such as Plymouth, Boston, Christchurch and Perth. The Mackenzie River in Canada is named after the Scottish explorer Alexander Mackenzie.

Annie Moore and her brothers were the first emigrants to pass through Ellis Island in New York harbour when it opened on 1st January 1892. They sailed from Ireland.

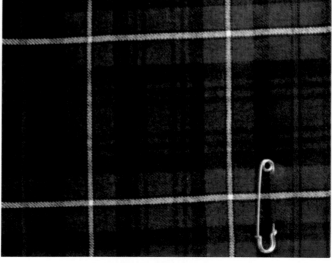

My dad, James (Jim) Erskine Henshelwood wearing the MacKenzie tartan.

Names, in particular first names and middle names were often — and still are - passed down through the generations of families as shown in Chapter 2, page 39.

In England names that end with the word 'son', like Williamson, Jackson and Robinson very probably at some time had fathers called William, Jack and Robin. Williamson would have been the 'son of William', Jackson the 'son of Jack' and so on. . .

You may have sometimes wondered why in Ireland there are names that begin with an 'O' such as O'Malley; and in Scotland many names begin with 'Mc' or 'Mac' as in McGregor or Mackenzie. The Irish 'O' usually means 'grandson of', whilst the 'Mc' along with the Welsh 'ap' both mean either 'descended from' or 'son of'.

In Scotland, especially in the Highlands, there are 'clans'. These are several families sharing the same surname, possibly living in the same area and having the same original ancestor. Each clan has a recognisable tartan. A tartan is usually a woollen material, with various patterns of stripes of different widths and colours, rather like the Burberry pattern to look at. Probably the only time that you will see a man or boy in a 'skirt' is when he is wearing a kilt. The kilt he wears will be the tartan of the clan to which he belongs.

When searching for someone in the records, be aware that people might have had their names abbreviated. For example, Bill may be recorded instead of William, and Maggie, Meg or Peggy written down instead of Margaret. Similarly people's nicknames could have sometimes been used. A modern example of this is the well-known cricketer Andrew Flintoff, who to most of us is better known as Freddie Flintoff.

Another pitfall that you could fall into was that some rich people not bothering to know the names of their servants merely gave them all the same name. So Phoebe, Ruby or Harriet could have all been called Alice by the master and mistress of the house; surely this must have caused much confusion, but avoided using the brain too much!

Yet another trap is one that we set ourselves when our eldest daughter, Abbie, was born. She is registered as Kate Abigail, but was called Abbie from the first day. She does get confused sometimes in the dentist's waiting-room when 'Kate' is called out.

You may discover that some families had more than one child with the same name. With careful detective work, you will probably discover that the first one had nearly always died. So many people died young because of poor, unhygienic living conditions and, the lack of good nursing care and medicines. It was also very common for mothers to die when they had their babies. If the babies did survive, they were still at risk from the common childhood diseases. Mass vaccination was not available then and antibiotics, which we now take for granted, were not invented until the 20th century. It is apparent from the death registers at my local register office, that there was a measles epidemic during the winter of 1837/1838. Name after name of young children appear, having died from "Infection after measles", with many of the informants (the mother or father) having signed with an **X**. This means that they were illiterate as mentioned in Chapter 4.

Have you ever heard of Florence Nightingale? She became famous for her nursing care during the Crimean War (1853-1856). She was given the nickname of 'The Lady of the Lamp' as she used a lamp to light her way round the wards when checking her patients at night.

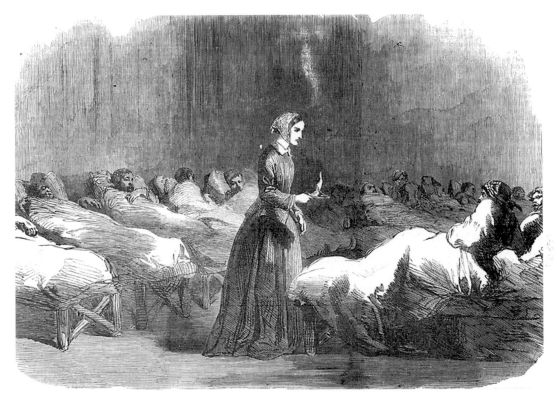

Florence Nightingale, the Lady of the Lamp.

It is a known fact that more men died in the Crimean War from cholera than from their wounds. Cholera is still a very dangerously infectious disease in poorer parts of the world today. People are frightened of catching it even now — rather like Aids and meningitis in our part of the world. Similarly the 1918-19 influenza (flu) outbreak killed more people than the whole of the First World War. As I write this, there is a worry that there could be a flu pandemic at any time. Currently the birds in the Far East are getting the blame by starting it all with their 'bird flu'.

We have seen that Florence Nightingale's nickname was **The Lady of the lamp**. Some others that you might have heard include:

Peeping Tom was a tailor who was the only person to peep at the naked Lady Godiva as she rode through the streets of Coventry on a horse. Legend tells us, that he then went blind.

Richard the Lionheart became King Richard the First. He earned this name because of his bravery when fighting the crusades, which were religious wars.

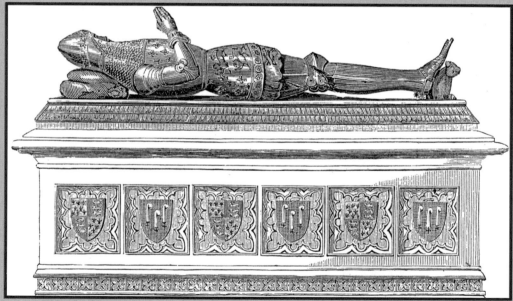

The Black Prince was the eldest son of King Edward the Third who wore black armour in battle.

The eldest daughter of King Henry the Eighth, Queen Mary, was called **Bloody Mary**. She ordered hundreds of people to be burnt alive at the stake (rather like Guy Fawkes on Bonfire Night).

Joan of Arc was a French peasant who became famous for leading the French army. She was also called the **Maid of Orleans**.

Blackbeard was the nickname given to this English pirate whose real name was Edward Teach. He got his name from his large black beard, and finally ended up killed, with his head decapitated and stuck on the bow of his own ship.

Bonnie Prince Charlie, born Charles Edward Stuart and also known as the **Young Pretender** fled to France after being defeated at the Battle of Culloden, Scotland.

In 1888, **Jack the Ripper** was feared around the East End of London for murdering several women. He was never caught, so his real identity was never known.

The Red Baron was a leading German fighter pilot in the First World War. Famous for flying a brightly decorated plane, his name was Baron Manfred Richthofen.

Twiggy who has modelled for Marks and Spencer was born Lesley Hornby.

We first knew of her as Victoria Adams. That was before this **Spice Girl** or **Posh Spice** married David Beckham (known as Becks) and mother of Brooklyn, Romeo and Cruz. The other Spice Girls were **Sporty, Scary, Ginger** and **Baby**.

Jamie Oliver, the well-known chef and father of Daisy Boo and Poppy Honey is also known as **The Naked Chef**.

Norman Cook is probably better known to most of us as **Fatboy Slim.**

Aunt Judy a younger sister of my Annie Florence grandmother died in 1918. She had been nursing wounded men from the war and caught flu. What totally confused my mother a few years ago was when I told her that Judy was given the name Gladys when she was born. Mum had never been told this, so here is another example of someone being called by another name.

A nickname (or pet name) often just 'happens' as a result of some specific characteristic, event or even joke. For example 'Ginger' is usually the name given to someone with ginger (red) hair. 'Paddy' is often an Irishman whilst 'Taffy' is normally a Welshman, and 'Jock' a Scotsman.

Perhaps you or some of your friends have been given a nickname. It is not only people that you like either, as in the case of the old matron at my school. As she seemed to be constantly snooping around she was very quickly given the nickname of 'Keyhole Kate!' A school friend of mine was nicknamed 'Spizzle', and what the poor girl, another friend in my class, did to be given the nickname of 'Skinny rats bloomers' I cannot remember!

There is in the West End of London a waiter completely unaware that he was given the nickname 'Titty Tickler' by flat-mate friend Anne and myself. Because the food was good we often went to his restaurant. You should have no difficulty in guessing what he was up to when helping us on with our coats!

I heard on the radio not long ago, that the most popular pet-name for a car is Betsy. A ship traditionally has a girl's name (although since 2002 many are now referred to as 'it' instead of 'she'), as do many lorries and trains. Even if a particular form of transport is not named, you will often hear them referred to as 'she' or 'old girl' (and maybe even worse if they have broken

Hannah Jane and Kate Abigail, two tractor units of the Eddie Stobart fleet of lorries. Thank you to Eddie Stobart Ltd. for the photograph and naming the lorries after our daughters.

TOWN and VILLAGE NAMES

You may agree with me that some of the following names are truly wonderful. Your street cred just might take a bit of a knock if you lived in one of them, although you would not have to own up to climbing Brown Willy (in Cornwall), or Great Cockup (in the Lake District)

Pity Me	Maggot's End
Pratts Bottom	Chipping Sodbury
Spital in the Street	Looe
Ugley	Wetwang
Nasty	Great Snoring
Ramsbottom	Lover
Mousehole	Giggleswick
Smoo	Waterloo
Peover	Bottoms
Puddletown	Wyre Piddle

'Starkies', a house in Bury, Lancashire.

This rose called 'Ancestry' was introduced in 1999 and has a pedigree (below).

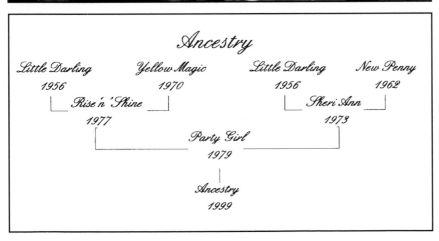

Ancestry

| Little Darling | Yellow Magic | Little Darling | New Penny |
| 1956 | 1970 | 1956 | 1962 |

Rise 'n 'Shine
1977

Sheri Ann
1973

Party Girl
1979

Ancestry
1999

122

down!) If you are an Eddie Stobart spotter you will know that every one of his fleet of over 600 lorries has a girl's name. Sorry, boys — you do not feature too much here … other than Thomas The Tank Engine and his friends.

Some children have imaginary friends with names. Both Julie, my sister, and daughter, Abbie did; we even had to lay a place for them at meal times.

Have you ever played the game of making names (and words as well) from car number plates whilst on a long car journey? It is quite a good way to pass the time and just may shut up that brother or sister, or even take their mind off feeling sick.

To take this a little further, the meaning of the word 'name' is a word by which a person or thing is known.

Most things have a name of some sort whether animals, trees, plants, roads, pubs, buildings and peoples' homes; even extraterrestrial objects like the planets Venus, Uranus, Mars and Pluto. I do wonder though why a Cornish fishing village has the name of 'Squeezy Belly Ally'?

Many everyday goods are named after their inventor; a favourite toy — the Chatter Telephone — was made by Herman Fisher and Irving Price. You may be more familiar with the name 'Fisher-Price'. Shops are often named after the person who started them such as 'Woolworth's', 'Boots' and 'Thomas Cook' (where you can book holidays). Two American brothers Richard and Maurice (known as Dick and Mac) are responsible for starting McDonalds, and the most famous toyshop in the world, *Hamleys*, was founded by William Hamley. It started off being called 'Noah's Ark', because

The 87 year old teddy in this photograph is called `Bobby'. He belonged to my mother-in-law and now lives with us. He appears somewhere else in this book. Can you find him?

"I'm Sidney Spider" and "I'm Millicent Mouse".

this was the only toy that was allowed on Sundays around the time of 1830. This Hamley family probably goes back to the time of the Battle of Hastings, as it is mentioned in Domesday Book although spelt 'Hamlyn'. This is just another example of how the spellings of names can vary over the years.

Some people name possessions after their children, and in one case I knew of a couple who named the family boat 'Vepasugi'. Their four girls were called Vera, Patricia, Susan and Gillian.

What made you give that favourite doll or teddy that particular name? Whatever it is, the little person has an identity and will probably be remembered more than one with no name.

Although it is more usual to give livestock numbers, all the cows and pigs on our Cornish farm had names. Priscilla the cow with her calf Bambi were the favourites of everyone.

You may like to know that for the year 2006, the most popular names for dogs were Charlie and Molly. Tigger and Molly were popular cats' names.

On a final note, talking of Tiggers, do you remember how Winnie the Pooh's friend Tigger became obsessed with his family tree? He was getting so upset that no other 'Tigger relations' could be found that Pooh, Piglet and friends all dressed up as Tiggers. I hope your friends do not have the need to resort to similar actions!

Important points to remember

❖ A maiden name (sometimes referred to as a maiden surname) is a woman's surname before marriage.
❖ An immigrant is a person who enters a country to live there.
❖ Migration is to move from one place to another.
❖ Emigration is to leave your home country.
❖ Pandemic means to spread over a very large area.
❖ An informant is the person who gives information.

. . . there was a Children's Crusade? As already mentioned a crusade is a religious war and this crusade took place in 1212. Thousands of children set out to conquer the Holy Land by love not force. There were two groups. A French shepherd boy called Stephen led the first; and the second was led by ten-year-old Nicholas from Germany. It was a disaster and most of the children ended up in captivity as slaves.

ALL THESE WORDS MEAN THE SAME THING

It is something that we all use everyday . . . what is it?

chamber pot   privy   thunderbox
jerry   latrine   jemima
convenience   gazunda   commode
throne   po   khazi (carzey)
the john   jakes   garde-robe
the sugar room   the necessary house
the closet of ease

In parts of Europe it is called Room 100

In Australia and New Zealand it's called the dunny.
The Israelites called it 'The House of Honor', and
the Ancient Egyptians 'The House of Morning'

FUN AND INTERESTING WEBSITES

Find out more about names at
www.behindthename.com
and www.spatial-literacy.org/UCLnames

www.movinghere.org.uk
tells us a lot about immigration to the UK over the last 200 years

CHAPTER 9

Every picture tells a story

It has often been said that, "A picture is worth a thousand words". Why spend ages trying to understand the writing, when an illustration will do just as well? Frequently though there are both, as in several places in this book; so I am hoping that if the writing fails to interest, you will at least have the pictures to look at.

When you think of pictures you may only think of drawings and paintings, but don't forget photographs. Have you found any 'old' photographs around your house? You may well find that more often than not there will be nothing written on the back of them. Sadly, this seems to have happened frequently and is extremely frustrating.

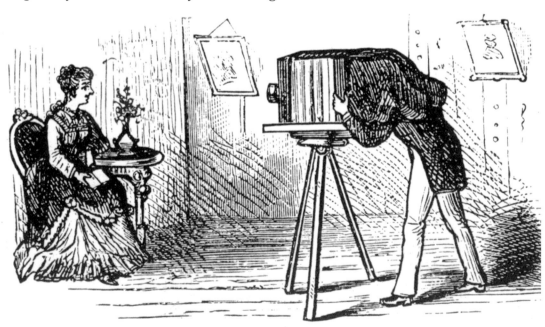

A Victorian photographer at work.

THE PHOTOGRAPH

As I was slowly ambling by
I heard my son suddenly cry
"Come, look at this, Dad over here"
As he pointed to a shop window near.

What flashed into my mind just then
Was a comic, a game, or perhaps just a pen.
And as I looked, to my surprise,
This is what had caught his eyes.

It was an old photograph in an old frame
All dusty and brown and without a name.
There was a father, mother, sister, brother
And a small baby on the knee of grandmother.

A sudden thought occurred to me there
I've a similar photo at home somewhere.
I searched through cupboard drawers in the attic
Not knowing I'd become a family history fanatic.

I found the photo I was looking for —
Two proud parents, sons, daughters and more,
And on the reverse in pencil was written
Everybody's name, yes, even the pet kitten.

And right in the centre sat grandmother small
Holding a baby in a baptismal shawl.
Her name was Sarah, and this rang a bell
As this was my grandmother's name as well.

I was so intrigued to find out more
I had to go and knock on Grandma's door.
"Where do these people fit in our family tree
And who is this child on the old lady's knee?"

My dear old gran aged eighty-seven
Said "All but one are now in heaven".
The only person still living, you see,
Is this tiny baby sat on the old lady's knee.

She said to me in a voice so low,
"The picture is of me 86 years ago;
I'm in the arms of my great-gran
She always was my number one fan".

I was still puzzled and I know why that was.
The photo was a lot older and it's all because
My grandma's mother was Sarah too
And the photograph's age was a hundred and two.

So there you have it, a six by four
Depicting four generations and more.
So search out your photos and do it today
Pencil the names on the back: don't throw them away.

By Peter Johnson

To avoid your descendants having to puzzle out who is who, before you forget, please write all the details (including dates) down on the backs of your own family photos, preferably in pencil.

It can often be the chance discovery of an old photograph that sets us off on the ancestor-hunting trail in the first place.

In some of the earlier photographs, the sitters (people in the photo) could not have been told to say 'cheese' as they do look incredibly fed up don't they? This is because it took far longer to actually take the photographs, and people had to sit incredibly still. Let's hope they were concentrating hard and not really the miserable old codgers that they appear to be!

Miserable looking old codger!

If you are able, you might like to make a pictorial record using photographs to go with your family tree. This will help your family history to become more interesting.

Most local libraries and record offices have large collections of local photographs.

The very first photograph was taken in 1826. Photography became popular very quickly with the wealthy Victorians. Before that, people had to rely on pencil, pen and ink or a paintbrush. As mentioned in Chapter 1, Henry the Eighth was not best pleased when he saw his fourth blushing bride for the first time. Perhaps the painter was trying to be kind to her, because in real life she was apparently very plain and unattractive.

As well as portraits of the aristocracy and the wealthy, many events in history were recorded this way. We will probably never know how accurate these sketches of the past are, but they do go a long way to helping our imaginations capture the moment. Another example of a picture of sorts is the 'sampler'. This is a piece of embroidered material that often has family names and dates on it. Occasionally they can be seen at antique fairs and shops. Some people still make them today, usually after the birth of a child.

"Threads of family history": an example of a modern sampler. Completed in 1995 by Glamorgan Family History Society.

Just as the written word, paintings and photographs record history, so do coats of arms.

There are several families today that still have a 'coat of arms'. They are very fortunate because they have a 'potted history' of their ancestors. To understand exactly what a coat of arms represents, you need to be able to identify the symbols and pictures. This code in pictures is better known as 'heraldry'.

A unicorn is to be seen fighting for Aslan in the film adapted from C.S. Lewis's book, *The Lion, The Witch and The Wardrobe*. We also see that Peter, the eldest boy, who went through the wardrobe with Susan, Edmund and Lucy into the land of *Narnia* is given a suit of armour for his protection during the fight between good and evil.

As you enter some towns you can see their coat of arms on a sign at the side of the road. At the time of the Millennium, a good many villages celebrated the event by putting up a heraldic type sign such as the illustrations shown here.

This amazing coat of arms of King James the First was discovered in Tom and Anne Feather's attic by workmen. Their house was built between 1560 and 1580 which was during the reign of Queen Elizabeth the First. The horn of the unicorn can be seen on the right and the tail of the lion is on the left looking a bit like a ponytail.

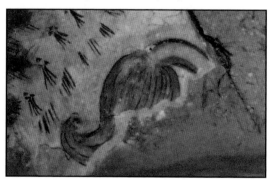 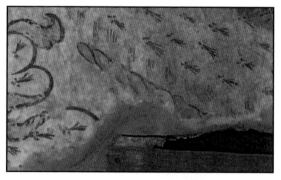

The enlarged sections of the photograph make the horn and tail much clearer.

I find heraldry fascinating and collect heraldic china if the place on it has any connection with my family. It is amazing how much information you can sometimes learn from just an illustration on a coat of arms. For example the colour blue often means water of some sort such as the sea or a river.

Heraldry was 'invented' so that during a battle you didn't accidentally kill someone from your own side! It had become increasingly difficult to recognise individual soldiers behind a

Village signs celebrating the millenium.

Thanks to Sheering Parish Council, the artist Heather Brown for Birchanger and Des Brandham for Hatfield Broad Oak.

helmet that covered the head and face. Heraldry caught on very quickly, having started during the reign of Henry the First (1100-1135). By the time we get to Richard the First (1189-1199 and known as Richard the Lionheart), there are the three lions of England on his shield. Coats of arms with their shields of wonderful designs in bright colours were easy to recognise, so showing and identifying your fellow soldiers . . . and team . . .

I don't think I will need to give any more hints before you suddenly realise where you can see these three lions as part of a logo! For all the inter-national rugby and football games and competitions, the England team strip

Above: Heraldic China.

Right: The 3 lions of England on a herald's tabard (short tunic).

Below: A heraldic bookplate.

Coat of arms with the motto *creo* which means 'Create and why not'.

Drawn by Myra Wilkins.

has on it those three lions. Teams not only wear their strip with pride, but we can see immediately which side has the ball.

Horse racing and cricket are just two other popular sports that have team or racing colours.

As well as the three lions, you might also have seen some flags and sportswear with the 'rose' of England logo printed on. Ireland has the 'harp' or a 'shamrock', Scotland has the 'thistle' or a 'red lion' while Wales has the 'red dragon' or 'three feathers'.

As mentioned in the Introduction, at both Olympic and Commonwealth Games, the countries taking part all have their own uniforms and flags. We can then see at a glance who and which country is in first place.

Flags are very much part of heraldry. Over the last few years we have seen a lot of the UK's flags, particularly the English flag of St George. We even see it on numerous occasions attached to car windows and painted onto people's faces.

Flag of the International Olympic Committee.

ENGLAND: Saint George's Cross

SCOTLAND: Saint Andrew's Cross

WALES: Y Ddraig Goch (The Red Dragon)

IRELAND: The Irish tricolour

Reproduced courtesy of Philip's Maps and Atlases.

The year 2002 was the year that the Queen celebrated her Golden Jubilee. I have already mentioned this in the Introduction, but it is worth briefly repeating here. Most of us will have seen the processions with horse drawn carriages, the uniforms and the waving of Union Flags.

Today anyone can apply to the College of Arms if they would like a personal coat of arms and if they believe that they are entitled to one. However it is not like going to a supermarket and selecting one off a shelf. Having one designed will take a long time and will be very expensive.

Heraldry is all around us, in places such as old churches, castles and stately homes.

However, many people are totally unaware that heraldry in a modern form is also all around us, although much of it does not resemble 'heraldry' as we know it. Nevertheless, logos and 'corporate identity' were designed for instant recognition in the present battlefield in the high street.

There are many places in our present world where this corporate identity can be seen.

The Arms of the Institute of Heraldic and Genealogical Studies. Reproduced by kind permission of the Trustees and Principal.

Above: The Midland, Derbyshire, photograph Elaine Gittins. Below left: The George pub sign, Hertfordshire, designed by Scott Wilson. Below right: A church window in Hatfield Broad Oak showing Saint George on the left.

- Hotel and pub signs
- Businesses and large firm logos, for example banks, building societies, department stores and oil companies
- Eddie Stobart, the road haulage firm, where all the drivers wear a uniform
- The armed forces
- The emergency services, the AA and RAC
- Schools, colleges and universities
- Travel firm logos, such as British Airways, Eurostar and P&O
- Town, country, county and principality signs
- Supermarkets, for example Sainsbury's, Tesco and Waitrose
- The Cubs, Scouts, Brownies and Guides (I understand that it is rather cool to be a Brownie at the moment)
- Formation signs on tanks and army vehicles in the modern battlefield

Most schools have some form of heraldry or the modern logo equivalent — I understand that the trendy term at the moment is pictogram. It can be seen in the uniform, the school badge and (back to sport) the PE kit. Even Hogwarts College has a coat of arms! Uniforms are easily recognisable in the local town, which sometimes can be very **un**helpful to those wearing it. My fellow school friends and myself were regularly reported for being seen in town without our hats on, and that meant detention!

Many schools have a 'house system' — again giving instant recognition. This is just as it sounds as the whole school is divided into 'houses' or groups. Each house has a name and they all compete with one another. At my school in Cornwall we had four houses, and not only did we compete in sporting and academic activities but also in behaviour. For good work and very good behaviour we were awarded with stars, and for the not so good, the punishment was a 'house-mark'. Three house-marks meant a detention usually at the weekend. Just in case you are wondering — yes, I have to own up to having had far more house-marks than stars!

Canting (or fun) heraldry. My maiden surname, Henshelwood, and my married surname Starkie on the right.

You can have quite a bit of fun drawing a shield and making up your own coat of arms using your surname. Why not design a Christmas card or make one for your grandparents' birthdays. They would probably love it and show it off on their mantelpiece or have it framed. Do not copy one that already exists without permission.

You need to be warned and made aware of something called 'bucket-shop heraldry'. Have you seen market stalls or tables at bazaars and summer fêtes selling coats of arms? You will be told that the one with your surname is your very own … but wait a minute …is it? The actual illustrations showing your name will be genuine. However unless you can **prove** that this is your coat of arms you are not entitled to use it. I have been into quite a few homes where the owner has proudly displayed on a wall what they think is the family coat of arms. I never have the heart to tell them that before you can claim it as yours, you must prove it. There must be many people with the same name that are not related, so how do you find out who is actually entitled to it? Well the way to find out is to compile a family tree!

Every 'picture' that you see, whether it is a photograph, painting or something heraldic, must have a story to it of some kind. Even a young child's attempt at drawing will mean something to them. They proudly tell us what or who it is, despite the fact that sometimes we cannot recognise a thing!

We are frequently told, "What you see is what you get" — WYSIWYG — and therefore 'Every picture tells a story'.

Important points to remember

❖ Remember to make a record of all photographs or write on the backs of them — in pencil.

❖ A sampler is a piece of embroidery (often framed) showing family details such as names and dates.

❖ Should you want to discover more about the fascinating subject of heraldry, there are several books on the subject. *How to be a Knight* by Sir Geoffrey de Lance is a fun pull-out book for younger children

Coat of Arms of the Birmingham and Midland Society for Genealogy and Heraldry.

The family history society for Staffordshire, Warwickshire and Worcestershire.

FUN AND INTERESTING WEBSITES

Look at some wonderful coats of arms at the College of Arms at:
www.college-of-arms.gov.uk
and www.show.me.uk
has lots of things to do including designing your own coat of arms.
This site has a link to the 24 hour Virtual Museum

DID YOU KNOW THAT ...

...... when swimming became popular in the late nineteenth century, it was frowned upon to be seen showing too much bare flesh! Despite the fact that people were almost dressed from head to foot, they would get changed in small huts on wheels (called bathing machines) that were pulled to the water's edge.

This photograph was taken in about 1935. The lady with the white top to her swimsuit is my grandmother, Annie Florence.

The photograph here showing a bathing machine was taken in about 1911 at Tenby, South Wales.

Not too much flesh showing here!

TREMENDOUS CROSSWORD

Across

1. Twinkle, twinkle little —— (4)
4. A Romany or tinker (5)
7. A puzzle that usually makes a picture (6)
10. Mums & dads (7)
12. A number (3)
14. Chose a child & legally became his or her parents (7)
16. Count of the population every 10 years (6)
18. —— upping takes place on the River Thames (4)
20. Edward —— was known as Blackbeard the pirate (5)
21. A worldwide chain of shops; a space or opening (3)
22. The opposite of open (6)
25. Jeans are made from this material (5)
26. A piece of embroidered material with names & dates (7)
28. A —— of arms (4)
30. The 3 —— can be seen on the English shield (5)
31. Replies to questions (7)
32. Press clothes or newspapers with this (4)
35. St. George is supposed to have slain this scaly monster (6)
36. Capital of Northern Ireland (7)
37. Curriculum Vitae [abbreviation] (2)
38. ——— Tom dared to look at Lady Godiva (7)
41. Excellent, cool & absolutely fabulous (7)
42. Weapon that killed King Harold in 1066 (5)
43. —— Fawkes (3)
44. He murdered Harry Potter's parents (9)
46. Taken daily at school (8)
52. Pizza or Hogwarts ———— (7)
53. Wicked people who lured ships onto rocks (8)
54. Convicts were ————— overseas (11)
58. Loud noise made while asleep (5)
60. Famous battle in 1066 (8)
63. A relative (5)
65. Florence Nightingale was the Lady of the —— (4)
69. The nickname of a queen was Bloody —— (4)
71. A sweep (often a young boy) cleaned it (7)
72. These keep you in touch by talking, texting & taking photos (7)
73. Friend or pal (4)
74. Building for teaching children (6)
75. Donkey or silly person (3)
77. Wild red flower worn on Remembrance Sunday; a girl's name (5)
79. The Earth or ——— Wide Web (5)
80. Item of underwear – definitely not a thong! (6)
81. School break time in the ——ground (4)
84. The country north of England (8)
87. Rearrange the word 'live' (or 'vile') (4)
89. Lots of hugs (7)
90. Music with flashing lights at party (5)
91. Vegetable at Hallowe'en or Cinderella's coach (7)
94. Great [txt] (3)
95. Cardiff is the capital of —— (5)
96. In your ———; not nightmares (6)
98. Sealed with a loving kiss [txt] (5)
100. ——— mail (5)
102. Either one thing — another (2)
104. Prisoners were kept here in the castle (7)
106. Soft toy bear or item of girls' underwear (5)
107. Secretly looked for top-secret information (5)
108. A metal can (3)
110. Foolish (5)
111. Famous admiral who died at the Battle of Trafalgar (6)
112. —— of Cleves was the fourth wife of Henry the Eighth (4)
115. Take in & look after others' children (6)
117. The National Archives [abbreviation] (3)
118. Opposite of hit (4)
120. Places (often free) to see collections of old things (7)
122. United States [abbreviation] (2)
123. Bone idle (4)
124. Short for 'William' or a legal document (4)

Down

1. The ———— in the cupboard (8)
2. Room at the top of a house (5)
3. 24 & 33 on page 76 make this farmyard sound (3)
4. Person legally responsible for a child (8)
5. Drink small amounts delicately (3)
6. Father (3)
8. —— & crossbones (5)
9. Wave this, or fly it from a tall pole (4)
10. Another word for family tree (8)
11. —— lots of questions (3)
13. Doctor —— (3)
15. Not even or unusual & peculiar (3)
17. Usually given at birth (4)
19. Mary Poppins was one (5)
23. Books are kept here (7)
24. Rearrange the word 'muggles' (7)
26. Bird that traditionally brings babies (5)
27. A sibling (6)
29. Pooh Bear, Piglet & Eyeore's striped friend (6)
33. Pupils in school used to write on this with chalk (5)
34. Armed force of the skies [abbreviation] (3)
36. Opposite of girls (4)
37. Someone who makes barrels (6)
38. A dish baked in pastry (3)
39. Blackbeard, Captain Hook & Long John Silver (7)
40. Rocking —— was a popular toy with wealthy children (5)
41. A behind or backside (3)
42. A fruit, or the daughter of Gwyneth Paltrow (5)
45. Soldiers do it; a month (5)
47. 'Must have' musical accessory (4)
48. Colour of birth certificates in England & Wales (3)
49. Your mother's mother or 'nan' (6)
50. Mark left by a healed wound (4)
51. Two words meaning 'pedigree' (6,4)
55. A census is held every —— years (3)
56. Buildings where goods are made (9)
57. Damage or ruin (5)
59. Work, career or trade (10)
61. Armed force that fights on land (4)
62. Chewing —— (3)
63. Mythical horse-like animal with one horn (7)
64. Board game with black & white squares (5)
66. 'Spam' spelt backwards (4)
67. 'Pets' spelt backwards (4)
68. Gran might have thought this Big —— a raincoat (3)
70. Armed force at sea (4)
74. Work for exams in this small room (5)
76. It spins a web (6)
78. 365 days in a —— (4)
82. Noah's —, a toy for Sunday (3)
83. Norman Cook is better known as 'Fatboy ——— ' (4)
85. Buildings used to defend in the past (7)
86. Capital of the Republic of Ireland (6)
88. Very Important Person [abbreviation] (3)
89. Used during a power cut or on a birthday cake (7)
90. You ——load on the computer (4)
92. Please write with this when near records & documents (6)
93. On guard & alert (4)
95. A marriage (7)
97. End of discussion [txt] (3)
99. Small furry creature that lives with a PC (5)
101. Information Technology [abbreviation] (2)
103. Do this under the mistletoe (4)
105. Silly smile (4)
108. Tender loving care [txt] (3)
109. New York [abbreviation] (2)
113. Make & keep careful —— (5)
114. Ta ta for now [txt] (4)
115. Very well known (6)
116. Parts of trees & plants underground (5)
119. A stink; —— a rat (5)
120. 'The Sound of ——— ' (5)
121. Network of walls or hedges to get lost in (4)

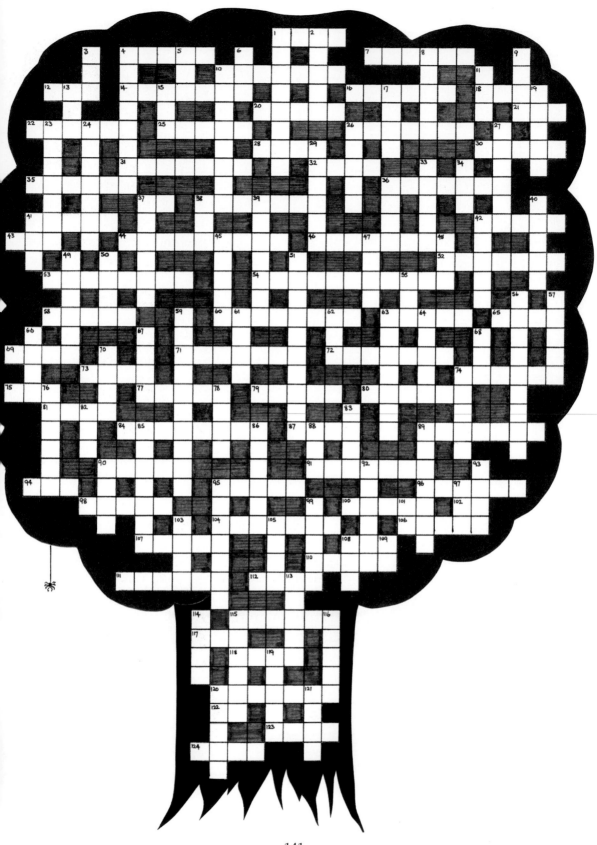

CHAPTER 10

This is your life

When I was a teenager I can remember adults saying, "Children should be seen and not heard". Well, words fail me even now! I was never impressed with that statement and have often wondered who had the right to say it. Yes, children should do as they are told and obey rules as long as they are reasonable demands or requests. This is for their own safety, and while they are under age, adults are responsible for them. To expect them to keep quiet all the time though and not make a sound — **never!**

"If adults were always right, the world would not be in the mess that it is in". I heard this quote recently and thought to myself, 'How true!'

We have had a very quick peep through the window to the past. Are you impressed that you may have been wearing the same clothes every single day and would have had no TVs, PCs and — absolute shock horror — no mobile phones?

The days have gone when most schoolboys had to wear their caps when out. There would have been no arguing. You did it, or the punishment might have been a few strokes with the cane.

It is true that some wealthy Victorian parents might not have seen too much of their children. There is a story that Queen Victoria was walking in the park with her husband Prince Albert. She realised that the children they could see playing happily were theirs, because she recognised the nanny!

Long gone are the days when children in the UK were treated badly and made to work for long hours in appalling conditions. It was mainly the young children, who were orphans or foundlings from the workhouses, that were made to sweep chimneys. Small people were needed to fit inside them. Charles Kingsley's book *The Water Babies* written in 1863 tells us about Tom the little chimney sweep who worked for Mr. Grimes. We have already talked about how children were disgracefully exploited in factories and other workplaces. An example from the 1861 census is 9 year old William Magee who was a factory hand. In the same year, 11 year old Sarah Dolan from Carlisle and her 9 year old brother James were both working in a cotton mill.

The Factory Girl's Last Day

'Twas on a winter's morning,
The weather wet and wild,
Three hours before the dawning
The father roused his child;
Her daily morsel bringing,
The darksome room he paced,
And cried, "The bell is ringing,
My hapless darling, haste!"

"Father, I'm up, but weary,
I scarce can reach the door,
And long the way and dreary,—
O carry me once more!
To help us we've no mother;
And you have no employ;
They killed my little brother,—
Like him I'll work and die!"

Her wasted form seemed nothing, —
The load was at his heart;
The sufferer he kept soothing
Till at the mill they part.
The overlooker met her,
As to her frame she crept,
And with his thong he beat her,
And cursed her as she wept.

Alas! What hours of horror
Made up her latest day;
In toil, and pain, and sorrow,
They slowly passed away:
It seemed, as she grew weaker,
The threads the oftener broke,
The rapid wheels ran quicker,
And heavier fell the stroke.

The sun had long descended
But night brought no repose;
Her day began and ended
As cruel tyrants chose.
At length a little neighbour
Her halfpenny she paid
To take her last hour's labour,
While by her frame she laid.

At last, the engine ceasing,
The captives homeward rushed;
She thought her strength increasing—
'Twas hope her spirits flushed:
She left, but oft she tarried,
She fell and rose no more,
Till, by her comrades carried,
She reached her father's door.

All night with tortured feeling,
He watched his speechless child;
While, close beside her kneeling,
She knew him not, nor smiled.
Again the factory's ringing
Her last perceptions tried;
When, from her straw-bed springing,
"'Tis time!" she shrieked, and died!

That night a chariot passed her,
While on the ground she lay;
The daughters of her master
An evening visit pay:
Their tender hearts were sighing
As negro wrongs were told, —
While the white slave lay dying,
Who earned their father's gold!

By Michael Thomas Sadler in 1820.

Children were treated badly and made to work for long hours in the factories in appalling conditions. Cruikshank's view of brutality in the mills.

Children going to work in Victorian times.

Preparing the master's bath. Photograph taken at Warwick Castle by the author.

Children with their nannies in the park.

Sometimes working in service for the rich families may not have been much better. Servants would have been expected to get up very early to stoke the fires in the cold months (this being the only sort of heating there was), clean the front steps, iron the master's newspaper (yes — honest! It apparently dried the ink and made the paper crisper), or put the water on the kitchen range (an old fashioned cooker) for his bath and the cook's early morning cup of tea. Putting the water on meant filling a very large and heavy kettle or pan, not flicking on an electric switch.

Not a very happy match seller.

Perhaps they were allowed a little time off on Sundays to go to church wearing their 'Sunday best' (if they had any best clothes), but as they were made to do this it could hardly have been a bundle of fun. In many households, Sunday was looked upon as a day of rest. Any kind of work was frowned upon and any kind of play or recreation was disapproved of as well.

It must have been a wonderful experience for servants when Bank Holidays began in 1879. With the invention of the motorcar, it was only a matter of time before all the staff would have piled into a large old-fashioned car or bus, and been driven off to the seaside for the day. This was the

A kitchen range (cooker).

From left to right, a warming pan, flat irons and a stone hot water bottle.

Left: visiting on Christmas Eve. Right: The attic room.

time when it was very fashionable for the rich to have holidays by the sea. The piers and penny arcades had started to become popular. Imagine the cars arriving from the towns full of wide-eyed, innocent and amazed young people who normally spent all their time seeing to the needs of others. They must have really believed that their dreams had come true … for a day.

In the 1920s and 1930s, if you heard a plane overhead, you would rush outside to look up because there were not many around and they were still very much a novelty.

Before the Second World War, only the wealthy would have had holidays abroad. It was not until many years afterwards that the annual holiday became popular. Up until then if you were lucky and could afford it, you

Best clothes for the Bank Holiday outing with the master and his lady.

might have gone to stay at a holiday resort in this country. You can imagine, that the first holiday abroad would have been a major expedition and experience, whereas nowadays people hop onto a plane and fly to almost anywhere in the world.

I am really hoping that now you have read this far, the last thing you are going to do is sit quietly waiting for information to come to you. I want you out there asking lots of questions, going to lots of places, making lots of notes and then writing it all down. Remember that if you have everything stored on a computer, make sure that you have back-up copies — preferably hand-written ones as well. Perhaps one day you will write a book, or a short story on the history of your family and the experiences that you had when researching it. Make sketches and take lots of photographs as well. If in any doubt — do absolutely everything, and don't throw any of it away.

Do beware though, there are many pitfalls and you **might** fall into them from time to time, so remember …

> ❖ Do not believe everything you see, read or hear.
> ❖ Do check the original documents where possible.
> ❖ Always read instructions and introductions in books.
> ❖ Watch out for different and alternative spellings.
> ❖ Keep back-up copies of everything that you do on the computer.

Having said all that, I hope you are still raring to go. This hobby might take you many years, as long as you do not sit down in front of a computer, copy it all out and accept that as the truth. I have warned you so many times about that, but hang on in there and do not be tempted.

The very good thing about Family History is that it's the sort of hobby that you can put down for a while, and then take up again later. This is where you can experience difficulties though, if you did not make careful notes. Believe me — if I cannot remember what I gave the family for supper last Thursday, how on earth will I remember which years I checked when trying to find the birth certificate of my great-grandmother!

When talking to people about family history I always ask them if they belong to a family history society. There is certainly no pressure to do so, but as I said in Chapter 1, I strongly recommend joining at least one if you can afford to — and that one would be the nearest to where you now live. This would enable you to attend meetings, listen to some interesting speakers and also to discuss your 'missing pieces' with other members. Nearly all societies publish four magazines a year. Certainly, if you wish, you can be a member of as many societies as you like, but this will become rather expensive. There are other downsides to joining these societies so far as you are concerned. Not only are many of the meetings held in the evening, but also the people that go to them you would probably describe as wrinklies! However the sight of lots of young, keen and eager faces would be very welcome so how about giving it a whirl and joining up! It would give you a wonderful excuse to stay up late. Having said that, I could hardly blame you for not being interested, as it is not quite the place for you to be seen to chill out! Perhaps you could persuade an adult to accompany you, or even better — go on your behalf!

I do stress again, that you do not have to go anywhere near any of these societies, but as also mentioned the family history fairs are well worth a visit.

Many of these family history societies and groups are members of The Federation of Family History Societies. This is a worldwide charitable organisation — a 'club of clubs' — that promotes the education of family history. A very well known society that you will also frequently hear about is the Society of Genealogists (SoG) in central London. The library at the SoG contains a unique and wonderful collection of family history material.

Family Reunion by Brian Gough.

A frequent question to family historians is "What started you off in the first place?" Whether it has always been a burning ambition to 'find' your ancestors, or a chance discovery of a diary, letter or photograph I wish you lots of luck.

Who knows, one day you could be organising a family gathering of 400 relations. This was the front-page story in a recent newspaper. Most of them had never met before and, quite a few had travelled from all over the world to be there—proving what a magical and magnetic pull this hobby has!

A family reunion at Farnham Castle, Surrey, in 2004. Their ancestor, a Bishop of Winchester, had lived there in early Victorian times. Reproduced courtesy of the Farnham Herald.

In Chapter 2 I tell you that everyone of us has a talent of some sort. A very well-known lady (I should say 'Dame') started researching her family tree 7 years ago. She has plenty of talent when it comes to sailing around the world on her own and, in record time. Her name — Ellen MacArthur.

I hope that your journey into the 'great unknown' of adding pieces to the jigsaw of your family history will give you much fun and excitement. I'd like to think that one day you would hand your work down to someone from the next generation. Whether this will be your children or others, it does not matter as long as all your hard work is not lost.

If you decide that you don't want to keep your work — **please** give it to someone else who would like it, or store it somewhere safe. It would be heartbreaking to think of all the precious information that you have collected so carefully being binned just because you've lost the plot! Imagine how gutted you'd be if you mislaid a really important piece of homework that had taken you hours and hours.

I have enjoyed writing this book and have learnt a lot. It has turned out to be much longer than I intended, because sometimes I found it difficult to stop! It is very easy to get hooked on family history — once you get the bug it is rather like a drug, but this drug will not do you any harm.

Your family history, if properly researched, is as good as everyone else's. It does not matter where you come from or who you are. You are who you are. ☺

Have u:

Kept careful notes?
Asked lots of questions?
Told someone what u
     discovered?
Enjoyed *ting ur fmly hstry?

1200
1212 Children's Crusade

1300
1314 Battle of Bannockburn (won by Robert the Bruce of Scotland)
1376 The Black Prince died

1400
1431 Joan of Arc burnt at the stake

1500
1538 Parish registers began
1540 Henry the 8th married Anne of Cleves
1553 Bloody Mary (Mary the 1st) became queen
1558 Queen Elizabeth the 1st became queen

1600
1603 King James the 1st became king
1620 Pilgrim Fathers set sail in the Mayflower
Transportation began (sent overseas in a prison ship)
1649 King Charles the 1st executed
1667 People had to be buried in a woollen shroud
1688 The 'warming pan' baby born

1700
1718 Blackbeard the pirate killed
1745 Bonnie Prince Charlie defeated at Battle of Culloden
1775–83 American War of Independence

1800
1805 Battle of Trafalgar
1811-1820 Regency Period with the 'mousy' hairdos
1826 The first photograph
1834 Start of the New Poor Law (as a result of this workhouses were started for the poor)
1837 Civil registration began in England and Wales
1841 The first census to survive (taken on 6th June)
1845-6 Irish potato famine
1849 Start of the Gold rush
1851 Census (taken on 30th March)
1854-6 The Crimean war
1855 Civil registration began in Scotland
1861 Census (taken on 7th April)
1864 Civil registration began in Ireland
1867 Dr Barnardo starts homes for abandoned children
1871 Census (taken on 2nd April)
1879 First Bank Holiday (29th May)
1880 Education compulsory (up to the age of 10)
1881 Census (taken on 3rd April)
1888 First murder by Jack the Ripper
1891 Census (taken on 5th April)
1899-1902 The Boer War (fought in South Africa)

1900
1900 Queen Elizabeth the Queen Mother born
Coca-Cola invented
1901 Queen Victoria died Census (taken on 31st March)
1902 Toy bears named 'Teddy Bears' (after American President Theodore [Teddy] Roosevelt refused to kill a bear cub)
1912 The Titanic sank Captain Scott reached South Pole
1914-1918 First World War
1918 Royal Air Force established Women (over 30) able to vote
1928 Mickey Mouse 'born' Penicillin discovered
1939-1945 Second World War
1952 King George the 6th died Princess Elizabeth became queen

GUESS THE ITEM OF CLOTHING . . .

. . . can you guess what it is?

long johns
bloomers
smalls
briefs
knickerbockers
drawers
pantaloons
combinations
passion killers

TIME-LINE SNAKE

To give you an idea of time in history, this time-line snake shows
many of the events mentioned in this book in their correct order.

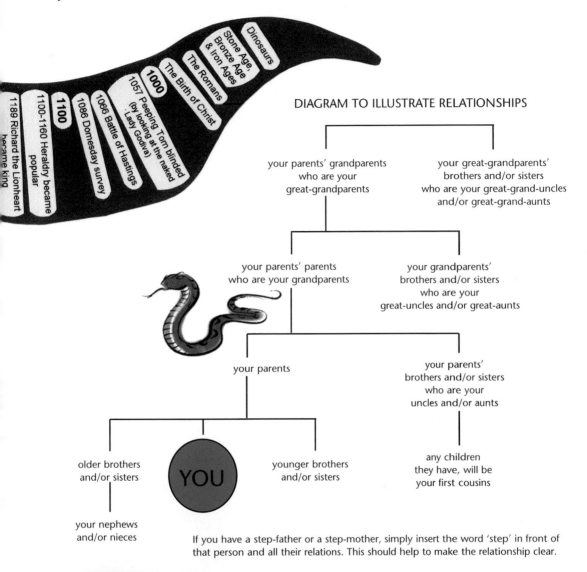

Dinosaurs

Stone Age,
Bronze Age
& Iron Ages

The Romans

The Birth of Christ

1000

1057 Peeping Tom blinded
(by looking at the naked
Lady Godiva)

1086 Domesday survey

1066 Battle of Hastings

1100

1100-1160 Heraldry became
popular

1189 Richard the Lionheart
became king

DIAGRAM TO ILLUSTRATE RELATIONSHIPS

your parents' grandparents
who are your
great-grandparents

your great-grandparents'
brothers and/or sisters
who are your great-grand-uncles
and/or great-grand-aunts

your parents' parents
who are your grandparents

your grandparents'
brothers and/or sisters
who are your
great-uncles and/or great-aunts

your parents

your parents'
brothers and/or sisters
who are your
uncles and/or aunts

older brothers
and/or sisters

YOU

younger brothers
and/or sisters

any children
they have, will be
your first cousins

your nephews
and/or nieces

If you have a step-father or a step-mother, simply insert the word 'step' in front of
that person and all their relations. This should help to make the relationship clear.

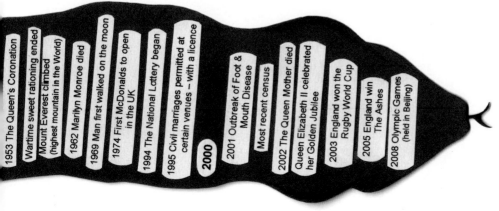

1953 The Queen's Coronation

Wartime sweet rationing ended

Mount Everest climbed
(highest mountain in the World)

1962 Marilyn Monroe died

1969 Man first walked on the moon

1974 First McDonalds to open
in the UK

1994 The National Lottery began

1995 Civil marriages permitted at
certain venues – with a licence

2000

2001 Outbreak of Foot &
Mouth Disease

Most recent census

2002 The Queen Mother died

Queen Elizabeth II celebrated
her Golden Jubilee

2003 England won the
Rugby World Cup

2005 England win
The Ashes

2008 Olympic Games
(held in Beijing)

Suggested further reading

How to Trace Your Family Tree by Kathy Chater
Introducing Family History by Stuart A. Raymond
Starting Out in Local History by Simon Fowler
Starting Your Family History by Margaret Ward
The Joys of Family History by Simon Fowler
Tracing Your Twentieth Century Family History by Stuart A.Raymond
An outline of Heraldry by Robert Innes-Smith
Learnabout Heraldry, a Ladybird Book by A.E.Priestley
Simple Heraldry by Iain Moncreiffe (cheerfully illustrated)

For the younger members of the family:
All about Me by Catherine Bruzzone
My family Tree Book by Catherine Bruzzone
How to be a Knight by Sir Geoffrey de Lance

Flo and Max reading aloud to each other.

Other books of interest

Jamaica Inn by Daphne Du Maurier — an exciting story that includes
   wreckers
My Story: Victorian Workhouse — the diary of Edith Lorrimer, England 1871 by
   Pamela Oldfield. This is one book of a whole series including other
   topics such as 'The Blitz', 'Transportation', 'Suffragettes', 'Mill Girl' and
   'The Mayflower'
Nobody's Child by Kate Adie
Powder Monkey by Paul Dowswell
Stone Cradle by Louise Doughty — is a story about gypsies
The War Years — The Home Front by Brian Moses
The Animal's War by Juliet Gardiner
The Children's War by Juliet Gardiner
The 2 books above have been written as Official Companions to the Imperial War
   Museum Exhibition
The Horrible Histories by Terry Deary
The Wreckers by Bella Bathurst
Twist of Gold by Michael Morpurgo—A story from the time of Ireland's
   potato famine
What I Believe by Alan Brown and Andrew Langley
The Worst Children's Jobs in History by Tony Robinson

The five fictional books below are about the Second World War:
Carrie's War by Nina Bawden
Friend or Foe by Michael Morpurgo
Goodnight Mister Tom by Michelle Magorian
The Amazing Story of Adolphus Tips by Michael Morpurgo (Based on a true story)
The Silver Sword by Ian Serraillier (This too is based on a true story)

For the older reader *World's End* by Donald James Wheal will give you a detailed
and true account of the Blitz in London and,
Children of War by Susan Goodman describing wartime through the eyes of children

The three fictional books below are about the First World War:
Private Peaceful by Michael Morpurgo
Remembrance by Theresa Breslin
War Horse by Michael Morpurgo

To continue with the First World War and again for the older reader *All Quiet on the
Western Front*. In this case the author is a German called Erich Maria Remarque
and the novel gives a German's viewpoint of the war.

Finally, another fictional book that was written in1928 by Lucy Maud Montgomery
called *Rilla of Ingleside*. This book deals very well with the true facts of the First
World War but written in Canada and from a Canadian viewpoint. Readers may be
more familiar with her first book in the series called *Anne of Green Gables*

Bibliography

Bibliography is a word that means other books — or a list of books — that I referred to when writing this book. It is normal to list titles (with the author's name) that are used to check information.

A Dictionary of Old Trades, Titles and Occupations by Colin Waters
Ancestral Trails by Mark D. Herber
A Nursery History of England by Elizabeth O'Neill
Britain at War — Air Raids by Martin Parsons
Debrett's Kings and Queens of Britain by David Williamson
Encyclopaedia Britannica (15th edition)
Harry Potter and the Philosopher's Stone by J.K.Rowling
How it all Began — Up the High Street by Maurice Baren
London Labour and the London Poor by Henry Mayhew
Matilda by Roald Dahl
Old England, a Pictorial Museum 1845
Reader's Digest Book of Facts
Reader's Digest Great Illustrated Dictionary
The Circus of Adventure by Enid Blyton
The Family Historian's Enquire Within by Pauline Saul
The Dangerous Book for Boys by Conn and Hal Iggulden
The Domesday Project by Elizabeth Hallam
The Guinness Book of Names by Leslie Dunkling
The Highland Clearances by Donald Gunn and Mari Spankie
The Leisure Hour 1861
The Lion, The Witch and The Wardrobe by C.S.Lewis
The Pan Book of Dates by Gerald Masters
The Ship of Adventure by Enid Blyton
The Story of Tracy Beaker by Jacqueline Wilson
The War Years —the home front by Brian Moses
The Worst Children's Jobs in History by Tony Robinson
Tracing your family history by Stella Colwell
Tracing your Twentieth Century Family History by Stuart A. Raymond
Wartime Cookbook by Anne & Brian Moses
Winter Holiday by Arthur Ransome

Address book

Federation of Family History Societies (FFHS),
PO Box 2425,
Coventry
CV5 6YX
Telephone: 07041 492032
website: www.ffhs.org.uk

General Register Office for England and Wales,
PO Box 2,
Southport,
Merseyside
PR8 2JD
Telephone: 0845 603 7788
Website: www.statistics.gov.uk/registration

General Register Office for Scotland (GROS),
New Register House,
3,West Register Street,
Edinburgh
EH1 3YT
Telephone: 0131 314 4433
Website: www.gro-scotland.gov.uk

General Register Office of Ireland,
Joyce House,
8-11, Lombard Street East,
Dublin 2
Ireland
Telephone: 003531 635 4000
Website: www.groireland.ie

General Register Office (Northern Ireland),
Oxford House,
49-55, Chichester Street,
Belfast
BT1 4HL
Telephone: 028 9025 2000
Website: www.groni.gov.uk

Public Record Office of Northern Ireland (PRONI),
66, Balmoral Avenue,
Belfast
BT9 6NY
Telephone: 028 9025 5905
Website: www.proni.gov.uk

Society of Genealogists (SOG),
14, Charterhouse Buildings,
Goswell Road,
London
EC1M 7BA
Telephone: 020 7251 8799
www.sog.org.uk

The National Archives (TNA),
Ruskin Avenue,
Kew,
Richmond,
Surrey
TW9 4DU
Telephone: 020 8876 3444
www.nationalarchives.gov.uk

The National Archives of Ireland,
Bishop Street,
Dublin 8
Telephone: 003531 4072300
www.nationalarchives.ie

The National Archives of Scotland (NAS),
HM General Register House,
2, Princes Street,
Edinburgh
EH1 3YY
Telephone: 0131 535 1334
Website: www.nas.gov.uk

The National Library of Wales,
Department of Manuscripts and Records,
Aberystwyth
SY23 3BU
Telephone: 01970 632800
Website: www.llgc.org.uk

Answers to the puzzles

Page 15 Anagrams
1. Sibling, 2. Records, 3. History, 4. Pedigree, 5. Ancestor, 6. Grandparents, 7. Adopted, 8. Census, 9. Genealogy, 10. Descendant

Page 42 Muddled meanings – match the clothes
1. i, 2. a, 3. f, 4. j, 5. h, 6. b, 7. d, 8. e, 9. c, 10. g

Page 51 Square Snake Puzzle
1. Uncle, 2. Enter, 3. Relations, 4. Sibling, 5. Generation, 6. Name, 7. Elastic, 8. Census, 9. Sob, 10. Birth, 11. History, 12. Yoga, 13. Ancestor, 14. Register, 15. Roots, 16. Strip, 17. Pedigree, 18. Engaged, 19. Death, 20. Harm, 21. Marriage, 22. Emma or Ella, 23. Attic, 24. CUL8R

Page 77 More anagrams
1. Relatives, 2. Foster, 3. Guardian, 4. Uncle, 5. Aunt, 6. Certificates, 7. Generation, 8. Family Tree, 9. Library, 10. Graveyard

Page 91 Muddled meanings – match the occupations
1. d, 2. c, 3. f, 4. h, 5. i, 6. j, 7. b, 8. a, 9. e, 10. g

Page 106 The school is Rugby School in Warwickshire

Page 110 Star Crossword
Across: 2. Top, 4. Party, 7. Ancestors, 10. Picnic, 12. Kings, 15. Sty 16. Hi, 17. Car, 21. Creepy, 22. Euro, 23. Markets, 25. Cinema, 27. Career, 28. Coach, 30. Hat, 31. Sleep, 33. Deep, 34. Escort, 35. Gossip, 37. Arch, 42. Den, 44. Orphans, 45. Photos, 46. Term, 47. Pony, 49. Records 51. MYOB, 52. Wizard, 54. Ugly, 55. Aunts, 56. Style, 60. Org, 62. Bliss, 63. Diary, 64. Sudan, 66. Baby, 67. Key, 68. Snap
Down: 1. Zoo, 2. Trace, 3. Potato, 5. Family, 6. Trainers, 8. Connect, 9. Servant, 11. Cherub, 13. Score, 14. Arms, 15. Sweets, 18. Friends, 19. Weapons, 20. Wig, 24. Ski, 26. Actors, 29. Hag, 30. History, 32. Po, 36. Peter Pan, 38. Romeo, 39. Holidays, 40. Spam, 41. Mayflower, 43. Shopping, 48. Noah, 50. Crusade, 51. May, 53. Daisy, 57. Toys, 58. London, 59. Gas, 61. Ruby, 62. Bib, 65. Nap

Page 125 Guess the object